Secrets of

Peak

Performers

Dan Kennedy, Bill Glazer, & Lee Milteer with the Peak Performers

Secrets of

Peak

Performers

Wealth Creating Strategies from the
World's Most Successful Entrepreneurs

V O L U M E   I

Published by Advantage, Charleston, South Carolina.
Member of Advantage Media Group.

ADVANTAGE is a registered trademark and the Advantage colophon is a trademark of Advantage Media Group, Inc.

Printed in the United States of America.

ISBN: 978-1-59932-110-3
LCCN: 2009925533

This publication is designed to provide accurate and authoritative information in regard to the subject matter covered. It is sold with the understanding that the publisher is not engaged in rendering legal, accounting, or other professional services. If legal advice or other expert assistance is required, the services of a competent professional person should be sought.

Most Advantage Media Group titles are available at special quantity discounts for bulk purchases for sales promotions, premiums, fundraising, and educational use. Special versions or book excerpts can also be created to fit specific needs.

For more information, please write: Special Markets, Advantage Media Group, P.O. Box 272, Charleston, SC 29402 or call 1.866.775.1696.

Visit us online at **advantagefamily**.com

Contents

Success Is a Verb

DAN S. KENNEDY

What exactly is "peak performance" and how do you achieve it?

While different people may have nuanced differences of opinion about the definition, I would insist that there are some absolutes here – and that absolute clarity in your mind about what it is essential to consistently achieving it. On a casual Sunday drive it's perfectly okay to wander around aimlessly. Not so here.

I own Standardbred racehorses and even drive professionally myself, in about 100 to 125 races a year. As owner or driver, I'm never disappointed by not winning or even failing to finish in the money when I know the horse has given his all and performed to the best of his potential. I can be mad as a wet hen, though, finishing second when I know the horse slacked a bit and could have won had he exerted himself to the max and gone all in. And not only do I know, the horses know. Some are diehard competitors, others are not so demanding of themselves. People are no different. You might have trouble articulating a perfect definition of peak performance, but you know when you are performing to the very best of your potential, and you know when you are not. **A peak performer is someone who insists on peak performance from himself.**

My definition, then, includes living up to your potential and doing whatever it is you are doing to the very best of your ability, while constantly working to expand and extend and strengthen that ability. I've long owned and taught a definition of a related item – "productivity" – as: measurable movement toward meaningful goals. If what you're doing isn't measurably moving you toward meaningful goals, it's not productivity. Just activity. You can run in place and be active.

Whatever your definition, you'll want to identify the factors that contribute to its achievement. For whatever it may be worth, here's my short list…

Conducive Environment
Physical Capability
Intellectual Capability
Information
Organization
Work
Leverage
Tolerance for Pain
Beneficial Association

Briefly, one by one…

Conducive Environment

How can you achieve peak performance if you insist on placing yourself in environments that are not conducive to it? If you take or make important business calls on your cell phone while also driving, eating, peeing or, heaven forbid, doing all three, there's no way you can perform at peak concentration, understanding, communication, and persuasion levels during that call. If you try writing, the work I do more of than anything else, where you can be interrupted, permit incoming calls, compulsively interrupt yourself to check e-mail, you cannot perform at peak levels of thought, creativity, or speed. And so on.

Most men (over age 30) wouldn't dream of trying to maintain an erection and have sex on a bed parked in the center strip of a busy freeway during rush hour, but they'll ask themselves to do vital and important work under similarly disadvantageous circumstances. I have long exercised militant control over my work environments and the access of others to me, and as a result seem to be more prolific and productive than any ten counterparts, to such an extent that "how Dan gets so much done" is constant cause of curiosity, rumor, and gossip. To others, my control of my environment is puzzling. I am puzzled by their persistent self-sabotage. Having said all that, peak performers do not require ideal conditions in order to perform well. In fact, a distinguishing characteristic is their determined effectiveness at creating good results even in the least conducive circumstances. After all, anyone can look good when everybody looks good. But they also strive to give themselves the advantage of conducive environment whenever possible, as often as possible.

Physical Capability

For about six or seven years I carried 240 to 250 pounds around with me. I'm not embarrassed about having been so far overweight; I'm not vain about my appearance. I'm embarrassed about having been so stupid. Going back further, for some years, I had a drinking problem and began most days hung over. Had I kept myself sober and reasonably thin and fit throughout my life, I imagine I'd be a billionaire instead of a multi-millionaire, gotten there a lot sooner, and arrived a lot healthier, likely to live longer to enjoy it. Far, far, far from smart was I. So. If you check into a Las Vegas hotel with a fully mirrored bathroom, step out of the shower, see through steam a gigantic naked butt and belly and scream in terror at the naked fat man who has broken into your room, or you drink excessively or otherwise self-medicate, or you smoke like a chimney, or you stay up all night playing X-Box, or engage in any other behavior damaging to your physical health and wellbeing, yakking about peak performance is asinine. Get a grip.

These days I'm often asked how I've lost all the weight and kept it off. Most of the people asking are hoping I know of some secret diet – a simple one, of course – or have secured a supply of magic fat-burning pills I might be willing to share. Sadly, no. I just don't eat much crap and eat a lot less of everything than I once did. Heck, if I was willing to exercise too, I could look like the always-shirtless Mathew McConaughey.

Intellectual Capability

I'm afraid our national I.Q. is declining, at an accelerated pace. It seems people either don't, won't, or can't think. Peak performance requires the ability to sort fact from opinion, information from ideas, important from trivial, urgent from merely annoying; to organize priorities; to make decisions and solve problems at a rapid pace; think creatively, outside industry norms, customary methodology, tradition, peer opinion; prepare persuasive arguments; see further than the end of the tip of your nose to foretell the second, third, fourth, and delayed consequences of current actions and proactively control future events and their impact on you, but also respond resiliently to all those you did not predict. (It's rarely the things we worry about that actually get us. It's the unexpected that blind-side us, and then it is how ably we respond to those that determine success.)

Intellectual capability is linked to intellectual *curiosity*. Most people are quite content knowing little about a few things, within a small, narrow, and comfortable realm; most people "can't find time" to read what comes their way, let alone seek more. The peak performers I know are voracious in acquiring, processing, storing and using, and thinking about a broad variety of information and diverse opinion, drawn from sources of obvious relevance to their businesses as well as from eclectic and surprising sources.

Sometimes someone will tell me, "I *never* read *fiction*," as if that's a badge of honor, a rejection of all that is trivial. I'm not impressed. If you haven't read *The Bridges of Madison County*, you'd best not be selling to women. If you haven't read Raymond Chandler or Robert Parker, you have missed important instruction on dialogue. If you haven't studied comic book characters, you have neglected an education contributing to many entrepreneurs' wealth, from Charles Atlas, Jack LaLanne and Arnold Schwarzenegger to Vince McMahon to mine.

If you only read, listen, and watch within narrow parameters, you can only think within narrow parameters, but life problems, business problems and the people you need to influence are diverse. Personally, of course, I read *The Wall Street Journal* and *Forbes*, but I also read *Rolling Stone* and *Mother Earth News* and *Cosmopolitan*. I read business books, but I also read mystery novels, literary fiction, as well as autobiographies and biographies, and each year, I start over with the A's and read the dictionary cover to cover. Economist and bestselling author Thomas Friedman, who travels extensively, is famous for his fascination for what cab drivers think. He could confine his input to his erudite academic peers' opinions, but it's doubtful he'd be a bestselling author. Two good, daily questions are: What do you know today that you didn't know yesterday? The other: What have you done today to strengthen your intellectual capability? The whole point is to learn and to lift *something*.

Information

Donald Trump reportedly rises every morning at 5:00 A.M. to read a stack of newspapers from New York and from other cities where his company has condominium, hotel, or resort projects.

Most people are constantly trying to do things without getting and using helpful information readily available – online, at the library, in books, through association. Fewer than 50% of the members of any industry or profession even read its own trade journals cover to cover, every month. When people begin projects and come and talk with me about them, it is immediately obvious they've done little or no "homework."

For example, the person starting a marketing campaign for a particular type of product or service to a particular audience who hasn't even bothered to "play prospect," answer competitors' advertisements, talk to their salespersons; hasn't bothered to go where his intended customers go – if boat owners, to a boat show; if chiropractors, to their convention; if truck drivers, to a truck stop's lunch counter. People who show no interest or regard for the history behind the business or industry they are in or the achievements they seek especially frustrate me.

I can very easily identify intelligent, responsible peak performers vs. dumb, lazy poor performers when they come to me to discuss their business projects: the poor performers only have questions, the high performers have information to give me as precursor to each question. As example, let's assume you are head coach of the Chicago Bears, scheduled to play the Dallas Cowboys this week, and you are fortunate enough to be able to consult with Bill Parcells in advance of the contest. You squander that opportunity and reveal much about yourself, if you sit down with Bill and ask: "How do I beat the Cowboys?" You reveal something very different about yourself, if you present Bill with information about the key match-ups of your players against theirs, notes from studious review of film from the last time the two teams played, the current injury reports, and then ask specific questions about how to beat the Cowboys. If you do the latter, you will get thoughtful, in-depth and valuable answers from Parcells. If you do the former, you'll probably get vague, general, clichéd answers: stop the run, protect against the big play, contain the quarterback. The quality of the answers you get not only depends on the quality of the questions you ask, but of the information on which you built your questions.

Organization

I'm *not* talking about a clean desk, nifty filing system, or possessing a Blackberry that can direct you to the nearest Starbucks anywhere in the world. I once fired one of the most neatly organized fellows I've ever encountered. In his daily appointment book, at 2:00 P.M. everyday, neatly written in for six months in advance, was his nap-time.

Time-blocking months ahead including important appointments with yourself is a very good technique. But not for naps.

Peak performers rarely get to work in a neat, sequential, step-by-step manner. It's my experience that the bigger the success, the messier the kitchen it's cooked up in. For that very reason, peak performers work at avoiding waste of time, energy, other resources, and place extraordinary demands on others to do the same. There's just no room for waste. Henry Kissinger noted that there could be no crisis in a particular week because his schedule was already full. I operate in much the same manner; everything is scheduled and timed, my communications with others are by appointments, and a major effort is made to keep me in a productive state as many minutes of every day as possible.

You have to find out what works best for you, and then exercise whatever control you must so you can work best. I work well in a home office – others must get away from their home. I am a "piler" not a "filer" – others are paralyzed by piles around them. This is all subjective, not objective. It's personal. But you can't kid yourself about it either; if you are too easily bounced around from one task to the next, one place to the next, one "fire" to the next, you can't ever get to peak performance. This entire chapter required only 45 minutes to write because, in 15 minutes of preparation, I created the list of factors as an outline and a shorter list of three key objectives to accomplish; because I worked straight through without interruption or distraction.

Organized effort requires both general and specific preparation. General preparation encompasses mental and physical fitness, creating a conducive environment, and so on; specific preparation requires stopping to think before working. People jump onto phone calls, rush to appointments, go into meetings, dash off e-mails with zero specific preparation, and wonder why they get such poor results. As exceptionally talented as he may be, Tiger Woods does not just hop out of bed thirty minutes before a tournament, gulp down OJ and a Pop-Tart®, hustle out to whatever course he's playing, and grab a club at random and swing, baby, swing. He might get away with it; you won't; and he's smart enough not to try. (John Daly does that, and has pretty much squandered his enormous talent and opportunities.)

Work

It's important to find work that is meaningful to you, that you get good at, and that, the majority of the time, you enjoy doing – because there's no way to achieve peak performance in anything without long hours of real, sleeves rolled up work. I have yet to meet anyone earning a seven figure income year after year or creating and sustaining peak success, prominence, and leadership in any field, business, the arts, sports, politics, without putting in more than forty hours a week more weeks than not, and without developing a strong work ethic and productive work habits. As a matter of fact, most peak performers I know have the line between work and play blurred, and typically prefer their work to activities of escape or leisure. (It's not insignificant that the newest U.S. President's wife, Michelle, has repeatedly, publicly complained about Barack's obsession with his work, long hours, travel, etc. placing a strain on their marriage – and she ain't seen nothing yet!) Obsession with work and peak performance go together.

If you consider that bad news, then, frankly, you're not going to achieve peak performance or success. If you consider it good news, that you can create work for yourself that you find far more interesting and rewarding than going fake-bowling with a "wee" game or trotting off to vacations every other week, then you likely have the psyche of the peak performer. The evidence of link between preference for work, peak performance, and peak success is presented by the countless numbers of very rich and celebrated leaders of their fields who continue working – hard – years after all financial reasons for doing so are retired; those who return after brief retirements. To name a few risks obscuring the fact that, actually, it's the majority of the leadership minority, but I'll do so anyway: in entertainment, Regis Philbin, Don Rickles (in their 80's, rich, nothing to prove), Seinfeld; in news, Mike Wallace; in sports, Bill Parcells, Joe Gibbs.

These days it's popular and trendy to try selling "the forty minute work-week" or "the lazy way to" – the idea that you can somehow delegate, outsource, and automate your entire life, magically separate accomplishment from effort. But this is not really new. The ad-man turned author Joe Karbo's bestselling book and highly successful full-page ad headlined "The Lazy Man's Way to Riches" is old; it ran decades ago. *The One-Minute Manager* was a bestseller quite a few years ago. People have always been enamored of this idea, which is just one more reason there is such a small percentage of people who are rich. Most such promoted promises are actually bait and switch. When you get past the headlines and hype, you'll find out that there's actually quite a bit of work involved in trying not to work! And if you sneak behind the curtain and observe the promoters of these ideas, you'll discover they are working a lot more than they publicly let on in order to sell their no-work plans. Bluntly, I think it's all green baloney.

Leverage

Nobody achieves peak performance or success just by work. Even if you worked non-stop 24/7, you'd still hit a wall. There are 8,760 hours in a year. If you turned every single one of those hours into $1,000 net income, you'd make a handy but not all that impressive $8.7 million before taxes, but, nobody can actually work that much, and precious few can average or exceed $1,000 an hour for every hour they work. It's not really a sensible plan.

Peak performers seek and create leverage as many different ways as they can, and there's no space here to lay them all out. The obvious includes leverage of knowledge, know-how, proprietary intellectual property, personality, reputation or brand; leverage of the aforementioned automation, delegation, outsourcing; leverage of money and credit. But the "micro" list features hundreds of different opportunities.

The late Joe Cossman, who I did some work with and became friends with late in his life, was a mail-order pioneer and a very astute businessman, who made over a million dollars from scratch with at least 10 different business start-ups, all based on the simple formula of "stealing" the unused leverage in others' inventions and products. Joe discovered that most manufacturers fall into making all their sales through only one to three avenues of distribution, so he would go and secure exclusive marketing rights to a worthy product for the avenues of distribution ignored or not understood by the maker. In each case, he secured these rights without putting a penny up-front, and under very favorable royalty terms, because the manufacturers thought they were giving up nothing of value. (Which, incidentally, loops back to my earlier comments about intellectual curiosity, or, in these cases, the price of lack of such curiosity.) In this manner, Joe took a pest control product being sold only to the military and through hardware stores and made it a winner in direct-response advertising. Most famously, he brought The Ant Farm® to market as a toy; it was originally sold by its maker to schools. Joe sidestepped all the costs of invention, patent, trademark, product development, making of molds, etc. and profited from leveraging that which already existed. His story is a powerful example of leverage, in this case, of marketing know-how.

Tolerance For Pain

This is an "x-factor" not customarily discussed in how-to-succeed literature, because it is considered discouraging or negative. It is what I call a never spoken truth. The super-successful develop very high tolerance for the stress of responsibility, the pressure of constant appearance of and management of problems, the coordination of the complex, the scars of conflict, and the disappointment and embarrassment of failure. They are willing to be Atlas with the entire world on their shoulders. Some even, perhaps perversely, enjoy it. There may be a fine and often crossed line between masochism and peak performance – in sports, in business, and elsewhere.

I mention this here in passing only to point out that any idea of somehow arriving at a place of peak performance, exceptional success, high authority, and substantial wealth without being bloodied, bruised, scarred, and challenged every step of the way and every day you are there, not just en-route, is fantasy. Mental toughness matters. And I would add that immunity to criticism – the secret to a strong and healthy self-image (which governs the limits of individual achievement), the requirement for essential risk, and the key emotional ingredient of resilience – is absolutely critical. Nothing is more crippling than hypersensitivity to others' opinions and a need for others' approval; there is nothing more empowering than self-approval.

Beneficial Association

Last on my list, the development of "circles" around you, that you can rely on for advice and counsel without interfering agenda, that you can get condensed information and ideas from, and that you can leverage, as a network, informally and formally. I discuss this at greater length in one of my books, *No B.S. Guide To Ruthless Management of People and Profits*, so I won't duplicate that effort here. **Suffice to say, there are two important assets every peak performer possesses:** one, a very short list of trusted advisors, friends, and allies he or she can call on and rely on; two, a very, very, very big and diverse Rolodex of contacts he or she can leverage, for almost any purpose, as sources of or connections to anything he or she needs. Over time some people have these things to whatever degree they occur organically, essentially, accidentally, and randomly. Peak performers strategically and deliberately develop them.

I'd be remiss if I omitted a brief commercial message. I am, above all else, a salesman with compulsion to sell when appropriate, and here it is definitely appropriate to mention the incredible opportunity afforded participants in our Glazer-Kennedy Insider's Circle PEAK PERFORMERS coaching and mastermind group, uniting entrepreneurs from all over the world with exceptional marketing acumen and a dedication to peak performance in an alliance, assisting each other with their businesses and their personal development at periodic group meetings facilitated by Bill Glazer and Lee Milteer. Also, to mention the networking and mastermind-association opportunities provided at the local level, in well over 100 cities throughout the U.S. and Canada, with our local chapters, facilitated by our independent business advisors. Information about both can be found at DanKennedy.com.

And there you have it, my short list of characteristics of peak performers. What should be evident is that I do not view peak performance as a state you arrive at, a competence you achieve, or a collection of skills and habits you develop, but as something you do.

To me, success is a verb.

DAN S. KENNEDY is a multi-millionaire serial entrepreneur, highly sought after and incredibly expensive business and direct marketing consultant and direct-response copywriter. He is the author of 13 business books and a popular speaker. Information about his books can be found at www.NoBSBooks.com. He is also a frequently published columnist, commenting on business and politics, at www.BusinessAndMedia.org. For Glazer-Kennedy Insider's Circle, Dan writes and edits three monthly newsletters, contributes to online media, and speaks at several major members' conferences per year. Further information can be found at www.DanKennedy.com.

Dan occasionally accepts interesting speaking engagements and new consulting or copywriting projects and clients. To contact the author directly, fax 602-269-3113 or write c/o Kennedy Inner Circle, Inc., 5818 N. 7th Street #103, Phoenix, Arizona 85014. (Please do not e-mail any of the websites. Mr. Kennedy does not receive, use, or respond to e-mail.)

You can access "The Most Incredible FREE Gift Ever" containing $613.91 of Pure Money-Making Information courtesy of Dan Kennedy and Bill Glazer can be found later in this book.

The "3" Ways I Know To MAXIMIZE Peak Performance

BILL GLAZER

I've been an entrepreneur all of my life. When I was a kid I had a small business that repaired bicycles. During the summers while in college I owned a "Sno-Cone" stand in a strip shopping center to make enough spending money to hold me over for the entire year while I attended school.

Later, I had other fast food businesses in several malls and for over thirty years I owned and operated the family menswear business that my father began. I grew that business to be one of the top ten most successful menswear stores in the United States and the most successful in Maryland until I exited retail in 2006.

Now, I'm best known as a marketing strategist and the guy who runs the exploding Glazer-Kennedy Insider's Circle™ (GKIC) business. In case you're not familiar with GKIC, it's **"THE PLACE Where Entrepreneurs Seeking Fast and Dramatic Growth, Greater Control, Independence, and Security Come Together."**

I referred to the GKIC business as "exploding" because we have experienced an 850% growth within the five years that Dan Kennedy and I have joined forces to build our iInformation mMarketing company, which consistsing of three monthly newsletters, multiple coaching programs, an extensive catalogue of money-making resources (available at glazer-kennedywebstore.com), two large national events, and over 100 GKIC chapters throughout North America and Canada.

I find that some of the most interesting questions that I am asked by GKIC members are NOT marketing related. In fact, I know Dan Kennedy also gets many similar questions. The most common non-marketing related question goes something like this:

"How do you get so much accomplished…all of the time?"

It's a fair question, and the reality of it is, I have three 'related' answers.

#1: WORK HARD-SMART!

The first thing that I do to get so much done is I work hard-smart! What does it mean to work hard-smart? Let me explain. I'm not ashamed to admit it; I actually work very hard and put many hours into my businesses. In fact, I find it quite interesting when people brag to me how little they work. These are the same people who are either not successful, will never reach a higher level of success, or are just plain lucky.

While I will admit that I attribute some of my success to luck, I have never counted on it and I certainly would never wait for it to happen. Instead, I put in the time and effort necessary to accomplish my objectives.

Putting in a 40, 50, or 60-hour work-week isn't the answer. It's making sure you use those hours effectively. Here's a little exercise for you to do in order to help you determine how to work hard-smart.

First, determine how much your time is worth? Are you a twenty dollar an hour person or a two thousand dollar an hour person? Most likely, you are somewhere in between.

Next, for an entire week, log all of your activities and put beside each one how long it took you to accomplish it. This is sometimes not easy to do, especially when you multi-task, but do the best job you can in approximating your time for each task.

Now, go back to each task and multiply what your time is worth by the amount of time it took you to accomplish it. I guess you've figured out where I'm going with this. Once you see how much it's costing you to accomplish each task, determine if it is the best use of your time or are you better off delegating or hiring someone else to accomplish the task so you can only spend your time doing those things where you are being compensated for what your time is worth.

That's why I would never cut my own grass or wash one of my cars. I can easily hire someone who is willing to work for much less than me to do those tasks. If I really enjoyed cutting grass as a hobby or found it therapeutic, well that's a different story. But, I don't...so I would never do it. The same holds true for tasks in my business. I try to spend as much of my time doing those tasks that can pay me how much my time is worth. In my company, it's primarily overseeing the marketing and creating online and offline copy that generates sales. This is what I mean when I refer to WORK HARD-SMART – not just working hard.

#2: SYSTEMATIZE

The next thing I do to get so much done is to Systematize whenever I can. After all, by definition, a System is a group of activities that when working together in the correct sequence, accomplishes an objective.

The funny thing is that you, and every business for that matter, have Systems. The problem is that most of them are either lousy or not thought out carefully. They just kind of happened. I remember when I was working in the family menswear stores my father implemented a System to stamp every receipt "paid." Years later, our cashiers had a point of sale computer system and a receipt could only be generated after it was paid, but we still stamped each receipt until one day a manager asked me why we were still doing it and I said, "Duh!" My manager was right; this was a System that was put into place that outlived its usefulness. Unfortunately, most businesses have Systems like these.

On the other hand, when Systems are properly utilized, they provide a massive amount of leverage. For example, I have been teaching entrepreneurs for years that they need a System to reactivate Lost Customers as they are some of the easiest Customers to get to return to a business.

At my menswear stores, we would place our customers who did not return within six months into a 4-Step Customer Reactivation Marketing Campaign consisting of three oversized postcards sent out two weeks apart and afterwards an outbound phone call was made. This System would routinely result in over 10% of our lost customers to return to our stores.

Another example of a System is the fulfillment of our deliverables at GKIC. Each month Dan Kennedy and I have a System to write portions of our newsletters and record our CD interviews. Once our parts are completed they are turned over to our marketing manager to facilitate them getting printed, duplicated, and then mailed. This is a System that allows everyone to achieve maximum efficiency.

The best part about these and all other Systems is that once they are created and perfected, they allow for peak performance of everyone involved.

#3: GETTING THINGS DONE THROUGH OTHERS

People are often curious about my management style. I tell them that it is very simple. My definition of management is getting things done through others. The truth is that you cannot ever grow your business or income without the help of others.

I don't care if you never have an employee; you still need to get things done through others. You might need to outsource or solicit the help of co-workers, but in order to grow and maximize your peak performance you've got to eventually delegate some of your tasks.

While more and more people seem to be going the route of virtual assistants these days, I guess I'm still old-school; I like to have employees around me. This is not to say that we don't outsource a lot of tasks such as printing and fulfillment, but as of the writing of this chapter, Glazer-Kennedy Insider's Circle™ and its affiliate companies employ approximately thirty employees.

Obviously we could never have enjoyed our growth without them. You can believe me when I tell you that I am not running a government agency at GKIC, where people are non-productive and oftentimes unnecessary. At GKIC you are busy from the beginning of the day to the end of the day or you are gone.

I am also a big believer in "delegating with accountability." By that, I mean that I delegate as much as I can to the appropriate person, but everything I delegate is done using a system that I learned from my management mentor and friend, Vince Zirpoli, who calls it SMART delegation. It's an acronym for:

S = Specific
M = Measurable
A = Attainable
R = Relevant
T = Time Bound

I never delegate anything that does not meet the above criteria, and as you can see there is a specific agreed-upon deadline as to when it will be accomplished.

PUTTING ALL THE PIECES TOGETHER

It should be obvious to you by now that each of "The 3 Ways I Know To Maximize Peak Performance" really works best when they all work together rather than separately. In fact, I believe it is really impossible not to have them working at the same time.

Think about it. You really need to figure out what you should be doing that is the best use of your time and then delegate to others what you should NOT be doing. Also, whether you or others are doing the task, it is best for everyone to Systematize as much as you can so the task can be created one time (and hopefully one time only) and repeated over and over again.

To accomplish this, it does take some hard work, but as you read at the beginning of this chapter, it is work that is hard-smart – my favorite kind of work!

> BILL GLAZER is one of the most celebrated marketing strategists in the world. He is best known for his OUTRAGEOULSY EFFECTIVE direct-response advertising and direct mail. In fact, in 2002, he won the prestigious RAC Award. This honor is equivalent in advertising as the Oscars are to movies and the Emmys to television. Bill teamed up with Marketing Guru Dan Kennedy in 2004 and they now provide marketing and business building advice to over 200,000 members and subscribers worldwide.

> You can access "The Most Incredible FREE Gift Ever" containing $613.91 of Pure Money-Making Information courtesy of Dan Kennedy and Bill Glazer later in this book.

Overcoming Unproductive Behavior

LEE MILTEER

As a performance and productivity coach I often hear people say: "I had this great idea but before I could act on it someone else did," or, "I learned something and I know that if I would take action I would benefit greatly, but I just haven't had the time to do what I need to do to utilize the knowledge, and with time I forget it."

As entrepreneurs, it is in our nature to see possibilities, but the main difference between successful and average income earners is the ability to take action even when things are not perfect. And let's be honest, when are things ever perfect? Economies and trends change quickly, and people who see opportunities and do not act on them quickly lose out, not only to the profits, but to the fact that competitors who have productive mindsets will take advantage of the new opportunities and changes to leverage their skills, services, and products to increase their own earnings.

So ask yourself right now, and be brutal about the truth: Do you have challenges, problems, and obstacles in your life due to the fact that you procrastinate on taking right actions, or do you allow circumstances to best you? How many good ideas, income streams, and market shares have you lost because of your unproductive attitudes and work habits? Will you admit to yourself that you could move toward the ultimate success you know you want and deserve but instead, you allow the negative news media to derail your plans? Do you let shiny objects or fearful attitudes distract you from taking risks and moving forward with your ideas and plans? Let's get honest with ourselves and admit we all could make more money, be more productive, improve our performance, and have a lot more time for fun, if we were more conscious of how we use our mental, emotional, physical, spiritual, and financial life energy. To be a real peak performer, one of the first things you must do is get real and get out of denial of where you spend your resources.

You must be mindful that the old saying, "Time is money," is true and you only have 1,440 minutes per day and 168 hours a week to manifest your life the way you want to live. You can replace everything except time. If you want to overcome unproductive behaviors, habits, and attitudes that have held you back, you must become brutally aware of how you are using your time and life energy. And even more importantly, what is the caliber of information you are allowing into your brain to program you daily of what is possible?

Remember this: We all have LIFE GIVING personal life habits such as exercising, eating right, and taking time to relax to reenergize our minds and bodies. In business, LIFE GIVING habits would be things like brainstorming in a coaching group for knowledge to attract new business and finding better ways to use your resources, marketing that brings you income, acquiring exceptional staff, updating technology skills, and looking for new avenues to expand your income streams without working harder.

We also have LIFE REMOVING personal life habits such as working too hard, not taking care of our bodies, not taking time with our loved ones, losing our temper, blaming others, negative thinking, excessive spending, overuse of mindless TV or computer time, procrastination, being late, and various other unwanted habits that detract you from enjoying life. Other Life Removing business habits would be spending too much time on email, not paying attention to what your staff is doing, thinking the past will equal the future, being closed minded about what is possible, pricing your services or products too low, not creating new products and services, trying to reinvent the wheel, or having unclear boundaries. Are you guilty of any of these?

Let me give you a big secret: first, admitting that you have the problem is part of the solution. Seeding your mind with other successful people's wisdom is, without doubt, one of the most important skills of success to overcome any unproductive behaviors or negative attitudes which have prevented you from becoming the creative, solution-oriented person you want to be, earning the money you want to earn, and living the type of lifestyle you want to live.

An important question you should ask yourself each month is: "What kinds of habits or behaviors do I have right now that serve me and which habits hurt me?" Knowledge is power when you know what works and what doesn't work. The first part of success is knowing what doesn't work and giving yourself permission to cut corners by seeking out people or resources that can easily offer you new intelligent and resourceful solutions.

The truth is, each one of your habits either makes you money or takes money out of your pocket. Think about it this way: habits are a way of doing something you have comfortably taken for granted. Everything you do becomes a habit. Your successes and failures come from your daily habits. Our past has reinforced our patterns of behavior, and it is difficult to change, even if we don't like the way things are. We are creatures of habit and these habits are familiar, easy, and routine. A change of habit means a disruption of emotional equilibrium. The new way of doing or thinking alters life's routine. We convince ourselves that it takes too much effort to change and that it is inconvenient because it takes too much energy.

You can no longer allow yourself to hang on to old traditions and ignore new ways of thinking. Whether you're trying to lose weight, swearing off cigarettes, kicking the procrastination habit, or marketing your business in a new way, it doesn't matter because you have the power to make these changes. Psychologists say that the resistance to change lies in the wall of inertia. Personality factors, like old habits and childhood programming, contribute to this resistance to change, and although you've spent your entire life becoming the person you are, you expect to change in a weekend. Let's face it: that is not going to happen. It takes from 21 to 28 consecutive days to program your mind to change and you need new resources to be able to have the knowledge and support to change unproductive habits.

The bottom line is that you need to first come clean with yourself and look in the mirror in your own eyes and admit to yourself where you have been in denial before. You need to give up blaming anyone or anything else! You and you alone are 100% responsible for your success. To be a real peak performer, you must give up all excuses you have used in the past and create a plan of action that will move you past any type of unproductive behaviors, thoughts, and attitudes.

Your thoughts, intentions, and actions create your future. YOU are self-fulfilling prophecies and what YOU focus on, YOU bring into your reality. So it's just common sense that you can empower yourself by realizing that you can choose a new response to any circumstance and thus, powerfully affect your future. Take responsibility for what you get in life and then you will have the power to alter any circumstance of your future.

You must accept that your actions or lack of actions have consequences and you must look at how your unproductive behaviors or habits have affected your business success, income, risk-taking, peace of mind, health, and family life.

There is a huge secret to making changes in your behaviors, thoughts, and actions. You simply must become conscious and then invest in a resource that will give you new references in your brain and the motivation and inspiration to make new changes in your life. A powerful resource that you might want to invest in is "The Overcoming Unproductive Behaviors System" I developed a few years ago after I helped one of my clients lose 100 pounds and start a new seven-figure business. I had so many folks ask how they could move past the negative habits and dragons that held them back, so I gathered all the information I have shared with my personal and business coaching clients and put it into a system that will give you the resources you need to make the changes that bring huge results. Go to www.unproductivehabits. com for more information on how this system can benefit your business and life.

Right now is your point of power! Give up old traditions that you follow out of habit, where you have surrendered your personal preferences for the kind of life you really want. The truth is that you have within you unlimited potential to make your dreams come true and to create the life you want. All Success has to be created internally before it can be created externally. You must accept your own personal power to create your life before you can make your vision, hopes, and dreams a reality. You must supply yourself with the motivation, passion, and excitement of what is possible. Without the essential ingredients of feeling powerful, you will not muster the necessary energy to inspire yourself to go for what you want and break free of your old, unproductive behaviors.

By taking responsibility for your thoughts and feelings, you choose to be proactive in life and not just let life happen to you. You do have the power today to transform your life by expanding your boundaries to claim for yourself new territories of the mind and what is possible. The bottom line is that no one can truly make you a success at what you want in life—no one but YOU! Invest in yourself and remember that you are a work in progress. Go for it!

LEE MILTEER is a professional speaker, author, and television personality. She is also a performance and productivity coach for the Millionaire Smarts™ Coaching Program for entrepreneurs and a Peak Performers Partner with Dan Kennedy and Bill Glazer. She is the author of *Success is an Inside Job* and *Spiritual Power Tools for Successful Selling* and coauthor of *Walking with the Wise for Entrepreneurs, Reach Your Career Dreams,* and *Walking with the Wise Overcoming Obstacles.* She has many educational CD and DVD programs, such as The OVERCOMING UNPRODUCTIVE BEHAVIORS SYSTEM, to assist you to reach your career and personal dreams.

Lee is not only a successful businesswoman she is also a talented artist. She is a photographer and painter who has shown and sold her work in galleries and art shows. Lee also enjoys reading, walking on the beach, and traveling. She lives in Virginia Beach, Virginia with her husband. Lee is available for limited speaking engagements and personal coaching clients. You can learn more about Lee at www.milteer.com.

Lee Milteer
2100 Thoroughgood Road
Virginia Beach VA 23455
757-363-5800
757-363-5801
www.milteer.com
office@milteer.com

FREE BONUS for you. Please visit www.milteer.com and download your free reports such as: Time Integrity for Entrepreneurs. While at the web site, be sure to sign up for my FREE weekly Smart Thinking e-newsletter to help you regain a sense of clarity and purpose, and reach your potential.

How to Incorporate the F-Word Into Your Business: Of Course I Am Talking About FAMOUS

ADAM WITTY

Throughout my entrepreneurial journey I have come across many rules and truisms. These include such popular rules of thumb like "no matter how long you think it will take, double it" and "80% of your profit comes from 20% of your customers." Of course, some of these truisms are more accurate than others. In particular, there is one rule that I have come to embrace, eternalize, and live by. The rule is: People buy people, not companies.

What do I mean by that? Simply put, people are attracted to other people – people have personalities, emotions, and characteristics. It is impossible for an inanimate object like a company to have feelings, personality, or emotion of any kind.

Nike embraced this principle early on, as the first athletic company to sign celebrity endorsers. What makes Nike famous? Not Nike, but Michael Jordan, Lebron James, and Tiger Woods.

Richard Branson, founder of Virgin understands this. Virgin has been a smashing success around the world in over 30 different businesses and industries because consumers are attracted to the personality of Richard Branson.

Personally, I only buy Dell computer equipment. Why? Because as an entrepreneur that started his first business out of a dorm room, I feel a special bond with Michael Dell. Of course, you probably know that Mr. Dell started Dell Computer from his University of Texas dorm room.

Consider Donald Trump as another example. *The* Donald, who is arguably the world's most famous business personality, is really *not* in the real estate business; he is in the *personality* business. Today, Trump is knee-high in the business of marketing himself, making himself a bigger celebrity and personality than ever before. Not surprisingly, the more famous Trump becomes, the quicker and easier his real estate projects sell. Buyers pay a premium for a Trump property simply because it has the Trump name. I know this, you know this, and believe me – Trump knows this!

You might be thinking, "Sounds great, but I am no Trump." Well, are you in business? Are you trying to bring new customers into your business?

By living the rule, "people buy people" you will be well on your way to emulating other successful entrepreneurs. One of the easiest ways to get people to buy YOU is by being famous. One of the easiest ways to become famous is by publishing a book.

For the record, Branson, Dell, and Trump are all published authors. In fact, Trump's 10 best-selling books have helped increase his fame even further.

I want to share with you four ways a book can make you famous which will directly result in growing your business and your income.

#1. Become a Darling of the Media: Get Your Fair Share of Media Coverage and Free Publicity

Many entrepreneurs daydream about being on Oprah, being profiled in *Inc.* magazine, or being the guest host of CNBC's "Power Lunch." At the very least, these same authors want to be featured in their industry trade journals and publications. For most entrepreneurs, all of the above remains just a dream. Why? Most folks don't realize it isn't about them. The media doesn't care about you; they only care about delivering good content to their readers, viewers, and listeners. They want a great story. A book can be a great story.

Sending press releases and hoping for coverage just doesn't cut it anymore. You have to give the news media something to talk about. A book is something for them to talk about. Reporters are looking for sources for their stories and interviews each and every day. In fact, radio alone interviews over 10,000 people every single day. You may ask yourself, why aren't they interviewing me? The simple reason is that you haven't given them a reason.

Being an author makes you an expert. It also makes you credibility. Reporters love interviewing credible experts for their stories, whether it's radio, TV, print, or online. Let me illustrate with an Advantage author, Jim Ziegler. Jim's main business is consulting to automobile dealers. In fact, Jim was recently the keynote speaker at the National Automotive Dealer Association conference. Perhaps more notably, Jim has been a monthly columnist in industry revered *Dealer Magazine* since October 1998 (the same year Jim released his book). Who do you think reads *Dealer Magazine*? Ding, ding, ding – you guessed correctly – owners of automobile dealerships the same people that hire Jim. By the way, Jim was an absolute unknown to *Dealer Magazine* until he mailed them a review copy of his book. The book ignited the spark that lead to his monthly column in the magazine.

Would you like to be writing a monthly article in your trade's largest journal? Don't you think it would be a lot easier to get business if you were a columnist in your industry's largest trade journal?

As Jim will be the first to tell you, outside of auto, nobody knows who he is, but inside of the auto industry, Jim is a rock star! In fact, he told me that the president of Ford Motor Company recently flew him up to Detroit on their corporate jet to consult with them. Who wouldn't want to be a rock star within their industry? No need to pose the question, as to whether or not you would like to consult for the largest company in your industry... and fly on their corporate jet to boot.

#2. A Book Is the Ultimate Business Card

When you meet with a prospect, what is the first thing you do when you sit down with that individual? You slide your business card across the table, right? I want you to start thinking about a book as your business card. Say something to the nature of, "Mr. Prospect, thank you so much for spending a few minutes with me today. I greatly appreciate you making time to meet with me and as a small token of my appreciation, I would like for you to have a copy of my latest book, just published by Advantage. I think you will really enjoy it."

Now, let us address the obvious. As soon as those words flow from your mouth and the book moves from you to the prospect, two BIG things happen immediately.

First, the prospect will straighten up in his chair and take great interest in everything that you have to say. Whereas initially the prospect may have viewed his time with you as a favor, as an author with a book your status immediately goes from unwanted pest to welcome guest.

Second, your prospect is now pre-sold on you before you even open your mouth.

The reason is simple; your book is the ultimate sales letter or brochure and it sells the prospect on why you're THE expert on your particular subject. Rather than the typical question of "What is your rate?" the prospect will move to questions like "Would you consider taking me on as a client?"

It is extremely important that you make sure one of the last pages of your book has ALL contact information for you and your business. This is the #1 most important page in an entire 300-page book. Advantage author Terry Weaver has done just this. Some might argue that the other 297 pages are irrelevant. The point is this book is his ultimate business card.

Rather than sliding a business card across the table, start sliding your book across the table instead. You will observe big changes.

#3. Acquire Clients, Be a Customer Magnet

Use a Book for Lead Generation

Many individuals and businesses use a book to generate new leads rather than using the "same as the other guy" ads. They use a book to generate only the most qualified leads.

Would you like to give a book to all of your customers and best prospects that would immediately point them right back to doing business with you? That book is YOUR book. Allow me to illustrate with an example.

Carl Sewell is the CEO of Sewell Automobile Companies in Dallas, Texas. In 1990, Carl penned a book titled *Customers for Life*. In the book, Carl describes in detail his company's "Ten Commandments of Customer Service." Any prospect that walks into a Sewell automobile dealership receives a complimentary copy of the book, even if they are just looking. Well, as you can imagine, many of those prospects read (or at least skim) the book and learn of Carl's "Ten Commandments of Customer Service." After reading the book, they realize they won't get better service anywhere else and purchase their vehicle from Sewell.

Interestingly, in 1990 when Sewell published the book, he had three dealerships in Dallas. Today, Sewell has 17 dealerships spread throughout Dallas, Fort Worth, San Antonio, Grapevine, and Plano. Do you think his book had anything to do with that success?

How can you leverage your own book to acquire clients? First, hold a client appreciation party, and provide a complimentary copy of your book as a parting gift. Second, personally deliver or mail a copy of your book to all of your best prospects. Finally, if you have a retail business, give a copy of your book to every serious customer that enters your doors. If Carl Sewell can do it, why can't you?

#4. A Book Creates Ultimate Credibility-Power and Celebrity-Power

Have you ever heard of Robert Kiyosaki of *Rich Dad, Poor Dad*? Robert has gone on to make a fortune in speaking, coaching, training, and, of course, his business and real estate interests. That said, it was Robert's original book *Rich Dad, Poor Dad* that made him famous. It was that book that made him the credible "go-to" expert.

How about Tim Ferris of *The 4-Hour Work Week*? Have you ever heard of him? Prior to the book, no one had a clue who Tim Ferris was. The book made him famous, the book has made him credible, and Tim has wisely used the book to his full advantage by booking highly paid speaking fees, getting top publicity in television, radio, and newsprint.

Both of these authors would be classified as celebrities. They have come to dominate their respective fields as experts and gurus. What bestowed this "guru" status upon them? You got it... a book!

I recently attended the Inc. 500 conference. For those that are not familiar, the Inc. 500 are the 500 fastest growing private companies in America. As you might imagine, they had an impressive lineup of keynote speakers. Out of curiosity, I counted how many of the 35 speakers were also published authors. Any guesses? 27 of the 35 speakers were also published authors. Many of the speakers were CEOs of multi-billion dollar companies.

A book also gives you ultimate "street credit." A book gives you expert and guru status. A book validates you as an authority.

Think Different

In closing, you might still be wondering how you can apply a book to your business. Some of the greatest business transformations of all time have occurred with the borrowed ideas from other businesses outside the primary one. Revolutionary concepts and borrowed ideas have created entire industries. Henry Ford became, at the time, the wealthiest man on earth by borrowing an idea from a Chicago meatpacking plant. A packaged foods manufacturer changed its entire system of manufacturing by copying the pit crews at an Indy race, generating an additional three hundred million dollars in profits in one year. Google became one of the largest IPOs in history by leveraging a simple idea.

May one of these ideas contained within this chapter be the **spark that changes *your* life and *your* business.**

ADAM WITTY likes to talk about the entrepreneurial spirit and the American dream. At the age of 19, he decided that it was high time to bring those dreams to life and started a business out of his dorm room. Today, Adam is the founder and chief executive officer of Charleston, South Carolina-based Advantage Media Group, a leading publisher of business, motivation, and self-help authors. What began just three years ago is now an international media company with over 225 authors around the world. Adam and Team Advantage have redefined and enriched the publishing experience for authors. He is the author of *21 Ways to Build Your Business with a Book* and co-author of *Click: The Ultimate Guide to Internet Marketing for Authors*. In addition, Adam serves as the President of the Author Inner Circle™ and Author Marketing Summit™. An in-demand speaker, teacher, and consultant on marketing and business development techniques for entrepreneurs and authors, he is a frequent guest on the acclaimed Extreme Entrepreneurship Tour and has been featured in *Investors Business Daily*, *Young Money Magazine*, and on ABC and FOX.

Would you like to learn 21 Uniquely Different Ways to Build Your Business with a Book? Would you like to learn how to write your book in less than 7 days? Visit **www.HowToUseA-Book.com** or call **1.866.775.1696 Ext. 103** and request your free copy of *21 Ways to Build Your Business With a Book*.

Do What You Say You're Going To Do!

Michael Gravette

Motivation and Self Help

When I was in the seventh grade, I had a history teacher by the name of "Army Joe" Williams. He was called that because he was in World War II and spiced his history lessons with a lot of war stories. One day in history class, "Army Joe" Williams said something that would influence me for the rest of my life. We had a homework assignment and I didn't complete it. When he asked me why I didn't do it, I said, "I meant to." He replied, "Meanin' to don't pick no cotton. You'll never become the person you should until you do what you say you're going to do." Those words buried themselves deep in my heart. Excuses would never again be a convenient substitute for not keeping my word.

Albert Camus, French author, philosopher, and Nobel Prize winner said, "Integrity has no need of rules." I agree with this. True integrity has no need for exceptions and no reason for excuses. And keeping your word starts with integrity.

In 1985, I made a bold statement to my wife. I said that I would never work for anyone again. I meant it and to me it was a vow. Now, when you make a statement like that, you will be tested. Nobody gets a free ride in this life, but, as long as you keep trying, no matter how many times you fail you will awaken a sleeping giant inside you and the bounty of the Universe will be within reach.

Later on, when my new business was in trouble and I needed to expand to survive and I had no money ($28 in my checking account), I received an unsolicited Discover card in the mail with a $1500 limit. This allowed me to place a classified ad in *USA Today* and quickly expand my wholesale business. I believe I received this help because of my determination to keep my vow to never work for anyone again.

Maybe you should not use the word promise anymore. I think it's lost some of its meaning by being overused and misused. Instead, don't make promises, make vows or pledges or take an oath. Use the word that is most powerful to you and let that represent what it means to give your word.

Later I decided to start importing stun guns so I could get a better price. I found a manufacturer, but also discovered you had to pay for the shipment up front. I didn't have the money to do that. I sent many faxes, using every argument I could think of and giving every assurance, asking for the stun guns to be sent first and I would wire the payment within 15 days. I had a lot of the stun guns pre-sold; I just needed to get them delivered to collect the money. Of course, the manufacturer in Korea was not eager to do this. I was a new business and this was my first order. However, I must have said something in one of my faxes that convinced him to take a chance on me. He agreed to send the stun guns and I would wire the money 15 days after receiving them.

When I received his fax, there was a great calmness that came over me. I knew that this was the beginning of something good. I was even more confident I would succeed. I received the stun guns and immediately placed phone calls to the customers who had committed to order. Okay, so nothing ever goes as planned. Practically everyone cut back on his order and some wanted 15-30 days to pay. I went ahead and filled the orders – I had no choice – and hoped enough money would get back to me in time to wire the payment when I said I would.

The 15 days passed very quickly. I wasn't going to make it. Everyone was telling me to just tell the manufacturer that I needed more time. After all, what was he going to do? I had the stun guns. But, I couldn't do that. I had given my word. I had no place to borrow the money. So, I quickly sold my car and was able to wire all the money on time. Because I did what I said I would do on my next order he gave me a full 30 days to pay and my business was off and running.

If you are in business or thinking of starting a business, trust is the most important thing you can develop and your word is the beginning of this trust and next to cash, the most important currency you can have. I don't see how a business can grow and prosper without trust. Your vendors and customers need to be able to trust you. They need to know that when you tell them something, they can take it to the bank. Do this, and you will always attract people who want to do business with you.

Sure, businesses are run by less then honorable people all the time. But, I truly believe you miss out on so many opportunities if you choose to take unethical shortcuts. Your growth may not be as quick if you choose the honorable way, but it will be longer lasting, with no limitations.

When you make an effort to keep your word, many virtues are called into play: integrity, loyalty, perseverance, sacrifice and courage. When you keep your word, against all obstacles, these virtues will become strong in you.

John F. Kennedy said, *"People of courage do what they must – in spite of personal consequences, in spite of obstacles and dangers and pressures – and that is the basis of all morality."*

In other words, if you want to be a good person, a person people want to do business with, then do what you must to keep your word. Never give it lightly, and when you give it, let nothing stop you from keeping it. There is no higher virtue.

There is a story of Roman named Marcus Atilius Regulus, a general in the First Punic Wars. During a battle against the Carthaginians he was captured. The Carthaginians, feeling they had the upper hand against Rome, wanted Regulus to take a message to the Roman senate asking them to surrender. They would let him do this only if he gave his word to return to Carthage. He did give his word and sailed to Rome. Once he arrived, Regulus encouraged the senate not to accept the surrender terms but to keep fighting the Carthaginians. He then said goodbye to his family and friends and returned to Carthage, where he was instantly put to death by being put inside a spiked barrel and rolled down a hill. Refusing to surrender, Rome defeated Carthage and become a dominant power in the Mediterranean.

Now, should you be willing to die before breaking your word. Well, that's up to you. The point is, giving your word should be the most serious thing you do and every effort should be taken to keep it from being broken. Keeping your word has to start with the most simple promises. When you meet a friend and say you will call them next week...make sure you call them. When you tell a customer that they will have their order by a certain date, make sure they receive the order on time. When you tell a vendor that the check is in the mail, make damn sure it's in the mail. When you tell someone you are going to be somewhere at a certain time, be there on time. If you're late, you are a liar. You did not keep your word.

Aeschylus, a Greek playwright, said, "It is not the oath that makes us believe the man, but the man the oath." Just because you promise to do something doesn't mean it's going to be believed unless you are known as a person who does what he says he's going to do.

Now, before you start making promises to others, you need to keep the promises you make to yourself. If you are going to practice keeping your word, practice on yourself first, not others. Keeping your word is not an old coat that you can take off and put on when it's convenient. Keeping your word must be who you are.

Keeping your promises to yourself builds self-esteem, eliminates stress, and gives you the spiritual strength and resolve to keep your promises to others. So, take care of yourself first. Look at this as sacred selfishness. You cannot do your best for others until you've done your best for yourself.

Is keeping your word an inner battle you can win? No! You can't win it. You will always find yourself in situations that prevent you from keeping your word. But that doesn't mean you should stop trying. There is no honor and glory in fighting a battle you know you can win. Honor and glory and the rewards come from fighting battles you know you cannot win. So, keep on fighting. If you never give up, you cannot fail.

If you want to be a peak performer, do this one thing. Keep your word and **do what you say you're going to do!**

MICHAEL GRAVETTE started wholesaling stun guns in 1986. Today, Safety Technology wholesales over 500 self-defense, hidden camera, and surveillance products and has over 4000 distributors. Safety Technology also builds websites for distributors and teaches Internet marketing exclusively to its distributors.

Michael Gravette
1867 Caravan Trail #105
Jacksonville, FL 32216
800-477-1739
904-720-0165
www.safetytechnology.com
michael@safetytechnology.com

For Free Catalogs of our products and Wholesale prices, please mention the *Secrets of Peak Performers* book and send request by fax (904-720-0651) or email (catalogs@ gunas.com) with your mailing address, email address and phone number.

Cultivating an Abundant Mentality

STEVE CLARK

What is your definition of abundance? Take out a sheet of paper and write down the answer to the question – what is abundance?

Is your definition about having, acquiring, and accumulating?

When I ask workshop participants to do this the overwhelming response has been about having, acquiring, and accumulating.

Let me kind of turn things upside down by giving you a different definition of abundance. Abundance is not about accumulating, acquiring, or having but instead it is about developing a spiritual sense of the limitlessness of it all.

Abundance is not about having but about being. It is about becoming. It is not a place or a destination; it is a process and a journey.

Abundance is simply a state. If it is not a place or destination that we go to; if it is a spiritual sense of the limitlessness of it all, then all we have to do is simply train our minds how to tune into it. It already exists. Abundance exists in the universe. It has always existed and will always exist. It may change and show itself in different tangible forms, but it has and will always exist.

This is what Einstein taught us. Everything that is created, everything that we have right now, everything that currently exists has always existed and will always exist. Matter can neither be created nor destroyed. Everything exists simultaneously. All we have to do is learn to tune into it.

Why is it then that in spite of the abundance in the universe most people struggle and experience lack in their lifestyle, relationships, physical health, mental and emotional development, and income and wealth accumulation?

The problems we experience, the lifestyle we lead, the quality of our relationships and our physical health – everything that happens to us – is because of our mental conditioning and subsequent behavior. Most of us have been negatively conditioned since childhood and told by well-meaning adult authority figures and role models what we cannot do and what our limitations are.

Psychologists tell us that as much as seventy-seven percent of all the mental messages and images that we have about ourselves are negative, counterproductive, and self-defeating. As a result of these programs and images, we erect mental barriers that become self-fulfilling prophecies that prevent us from being blessed and experiencing abundance. We sabotage ourselves by creating our own walls and our own barriers. Stephen Covey, author of *The 7 Habits of Highly Successful People*, says it this way, "We do not see life as it is, we say life as we are." Our life experience is a reflection of what's inside us.

For thirty years I have made a habit of observing people and listening to their language. What people say when they open their mouth reveals a lot. It reveals who they are, what their programming is, what behaviors they will or will not engage in, and ultimately it foretells their future. People literally talk themselves into the future.

Here are some examples of negative, counterproductive, and self-defeating messages that people say to themselves. Are you guilty of saying any of these?

Buyers aren't spending money
The economy is really slow
I can't remember names
I can't seem to get organized
I can't seem to lose weight
I can't seem to find time to exercise
Nobody in my family has ever become rich
I can't seem to get ahead
People are really rude
I don't have time to read and study
I can't afford it
Nobody is buying
I never have enough time
I just don't have the patience for that
Another blue Monday
That really makes me mad

When you say or think any of these or any other thoughts you are sending a message to the subconscious that says make that come true.

Recently, I was conducting a seminar when one of the participants approached me at the break and said, "I just seem to be having so much trouble. I'm struggling so much." I said to him, "Yes, and you're going to continue to struggle until you change that language because that language, that conscious thought, directs the subconscious to go to work and transform that thought into a physical reality. It says to the subconscious, got it? Got that picture? Let's go to work to make that one come true. The captain of the ship, the conscious mind, says I struggle. The guy down in the engine room, the subconscious, says okay let's make it happen. If you want to change your life experience then change your language, change your thoughts and you'll change your beliefs. Sow a thought, reap an action. Sow an action, reap a habit. Sow a habit and reap a destiny. It all starts with the thought process. Thought processes create habits that produce results."

Most psychologists would agree that less than 5% of our daily behavior is conscious and more than 95% of our daily behavior is automatic and is controlled by the subconscious. For example, we drive from home to work without ever remembering going through traffic lights or having to think about the route because we have done it so many times. Same thing with driving a manual transmission vehicle. Do you remember when you first learned to drive a manual transmission? It was like which foot goes where. Now, after thousands of hours of practice and mental conditioning, you can drive, eat a cheeseburger, listen to the radio, and talk on the cell phone, and shift gears, all at the same time without ever thinking about it. It's a conditioned response that is controlled by the subconscious, which governs our whole behavioral process.

What is the difference between the conscious and the subconscious? The conscious mind plants thoughts and ideas into the subconscious.

It is a mental thermostat that each of us has the ability and responsibility to set wherever we choose.

The subconscious accepts the messages from the conscious at face value. It does not evaluate those messages for accuracy and reality. It does not distinguish between right and wrong or moral and immoral, truth and fiction. It doesn't even question the validity of messages it receives. It simply does what it is told.

If we are going to experience abundance we must learn new ways of thinking and discipline our mind to focus on what is possible instead of what is not possible. We must learn to focus on what we want not what we don't want.

This transformation starts with a decision to focus on abundance and possibilities instead of scarcity and lack. Once we make this decision we must discipline our mind to stay focused and protect ourselves and our thoughts from those sources that would otherwise contaminate and poison us. That means turning off the television and minimizing our exposure to media sources that constantly promote doom and gloom. It may mean eliminating some personal and professional relationships that are toxic and counterproductive to our well-being. It may mean changing jobs. And in some instances it may mean minimizing contact with family members. In extreme cases it may mean getting rid of a spouse.

The scriptures address this very well. "Be not conformed to this world but be ye transformed by the renewing of your mind that you may prove what is acceptable and perfect and good in the will of God." Romans 12:2. The key word there being transformed. We are talking about a mental transformation. How long does it take to make a mental transformation? About as long as it takes to learn not to touch a hot stove.

That transformation can happen in an instant. Whatever we are dealing with, whatever issue we have, we can literally be transformed in an instant. But before this can happen we must make a conscious decision to, in fact, seek mental transformation.

Take inventory of your current belief system. What does your current belief system look like? Do you see and speak of possibilities or do you see and speak only of lack, problems, and obstacles? Get real with yourself. This may be painful because the truth often hurts. Pay attention to your language. What are you saying when you open your mouth? What do you say when you talk to yourself?

I would like you to stop reading and do an exercise. Take out a sheet of paper and write down ten things that you are thankful for. Because it is impossible for the human mind to have two simultaneous thoughts, you cannot do this exercise and have scarcity thinking at the same time. Look at your list. How are you feeling at this moment? What do you think the outcome would be if you did this exercise during the first hour of each day? Do you think you might start each day with positive expectations? What do you think the outcome would be if you did this every day for a week, a month, a year? I can tell you from experience that it would change your life like it changed mine. If you doubt this let me give you some quotes that helped convince me of this.

"Who so ever shall say unto this mountain be thou removed and cast into the sea and shall have no doubt in his heart but shall believe that those things which he sayeth shall come to pass he shall have what he sayeth," Mark 11:24. Here's another one, Matthew 7:7, "Ask and it will be given unto you, seek and you will find. Knock and the door will be opened unto you." Also Job 22:28, "Thou shall decree a thing and it shall be established unto you."

Say what it is you want, not what you don't want. Focus on what you want not what you don't want. Don't worry about all the other stuff. Stuff happens – it's always going to happen. Decide what it is that you want, create a written plan to obtain it, keep your eye on the mark, and execute and implement the plan with a positive expectancy that it will happen. If you do this you will increase your chances of experiencing abundance and a life of your dreams.

STEVE CLARK is North America's number one sales coach. He is the founder and CEO of New School Selling, an international business development and marketing consulting firm. Since 1980, he has sold pest control services, pots and pans, security systems, vitamins, laundry detergent, life and health insurance, annuities, mutual funds, stocks and bonds and school service products. He is a risk taker and an entrepreneur. In 1996, Steve was making $53,000 per year as a salesperson and he had over $40,000 of credit card debt. Taking out a second mortgage on his house and borrowing $10,000 from his mother, he set out into the world of sales and marketing consulting with zero clients, zero income, a wife and two daughters aged 10 and 13. It was a gutsy leap of faith that has paid big dividends! Today he earns more in a month than he used to earn in a year and the thing he loves to do more than anything else is to teach other sales executives how to do the same. In addition to his duties as a CEO, he is a US Coast Guard captain and runs a fishing charter business out of Navarre, Florida where many nights you'll find him 90 miles offshore hauling in yellow fin tuna.

Seven Steps to Make the American Dream a Reality in Your Life

MIKE ROOT

D o you buy into the American Dream that working hard can create a better life for you and your family? Do you put in those long hours to get ahead only to find that as each year passes you're no better off than the previous year? Isn't it frustrating when circumstances beyond your control like the economy or some bureaucracy actually put you further from your goals? Does this then make you feel burnt out or no longer motivated due to the stress of the task or the lack of progress towards your goals?

If this sounds like something you can relate to, this chapter will be extremely valuable to you, because this chapter will help you identify how to take what you know and turn it into peak performance. It will help reset your path to the American Dream by helping you refocus your efforts on productive behaviors.

As founder of a fast growing furniture retailer, I have lived the life of extremely long hours and hard work with small rewards. As they say "retail is detail" and I was involved in all of it. Working 70 plus hours a week, I didn't consider or know what a peak performer's life might look like, but I knew for a fact I was not living it. I was burnt out and all aspects of my lifestyle reflected this frustration.

The hardest part of any change is to admit to yourself and others that what you are doing is not working. For those of us who are entrepreneurs, we have personal capital tied up in the identity of the business. It is often times harder to look elsewhere because your company is your universe. For those working for someone else, you learn the ropes and the personalities in the company. A sort of comfort level settles in that lulls you into staying in an environment long past the time you should have moved on.

In either the case of working for yourself or someone else, when you realize that you are no longer satisfied with your role or you are no longer making progress towards your personal goals, it is time for a change. That change can occur within the operation or by finding a new opportunity in a different place. To transition properly, plan a new direction using the following seven steps.

1. **The Key to Success is to Love What You Do** – It is so much easier to feel good about your accomplishments when you do something that is self-satisfying. If you love what you do, work does not feel like work. It's a calling or a vocation that helps define your life. By working in an occupation and in an environment you truly enjoy, your whole being is engaged and you will meet with great success.

2. **Focus on Your Core Competencies** – You cannot be all things to all people. Each of us has certain skills or talents that we are better at than others. When you design your life and, consequently, your work around what you are good at doing, you will realize

your greatest reward. You either hire out or outsource work you don't like or are not good at doing.

This works very well for business operations as well. The businesses that are focused on being the best in their category are much more effective than those that try to please everyone. For example, instead of being all things to all people, we concentrated all our sales efforts on a certain type of account and outsourced the rest. It sounds counterintuitive but by giving away business we actually grew our business in a recessionary year by over 40%. We provided our core group with better service by concentrating on their needs.

3. **Peak Performance Is a Learned Trait** – Always be learning whether from books, magazines, training programs, seminars, or experiential opportunities. Be prepared to record your ideas with paper or recorder because you never know when an inspiration may occur that could be a breakthrough for you or your business. My kids lovingly refer to my vehicle as the "Knowledge Capsule" because there is always some form of informational CD playing whenever anyone gets in the car. The key is to always be looking for new ideas and then figuring out how to apply these concepts to your circumstances.

4. **Break the Mold of Your Traditional Business Through Networking** – Do you get so wrapped up in your own company or your own industry that you don't realize there are actually other businesses and industries where people make money? Unless you are out job hunting, you may never know about the remarkable businesses in your own communities that are creating value for society and profits for their owners. By taking

the time to network with other likeminded individuals, you will get major breakthroughs to apply to your own business. Through the Glazer Kennedy Insider's Club, there are a number of local and national networking opportunities. I myself joined the Peak Performers Mastermind Group in 2007 and have continued to see amazing results because of it.

5. **Add Value to All Relationships and Rewards Will Follow** – In 2008, I launched a new business called the Furniture Insider's Club (www.furnitureinsidersclub.com). Applying the successes that entrepreneur marketers such as Dan Kennedy and Bill Glazer teach, I wanted to apply these ideas with the business community I knew so well. My sole purpose was to bring many of the incredible marketing ideas I discovered to the furniture industry so that I could help others get the remarkable transformations in their business that I have seen in mine. Not only has there been interest in the awesome marketing ideas I present to retailers at no charge, my core business has improved. Customers appreciate the extra effort I give them with ideas and they want to reciprocate. Additionally, by taking the time to study new marketing concepts, I improve my business through applying what I teach.

6. **Speed to Market Is Critical for Success** – When the Furniture Insider's Club was started, a very important component was to take action. The objective was to get started as fast as possible and learn based on input from the marketplace rather than worry about immediate success or failure. What's interesting about the Furniture Insider's Club is it was started in 60 days without adding a single employee. The Power of the Peak

Performer Associations provided references for a very capable web designer, a copywriter, and backroom support. Most importantly, it could start quick, test the ideas, and change as need be without a huge overhead commitment.

7. **Always Be Marketing** – No matter if you are a one-person service business, a small business owner employing several hundred, or an employee in a large corporation, you need to make sure people know what you offer. Traditional media like TV, radio, and print is expensive and the results are not very trackable. Peak performers know that the real opportunities lie in direct response type marketing. From direct mail to websites to text messaging and many more strategies, multiple coordinated marketing mechanisms are critical for success in today's over advertised world. These strategies can work on the individual level all the way up to large corporations needing to get the right message to their target audience. More information on this very important topic of marketing can be found at www.MikeRoot. com.

Peak performance is a continual journey that is enhanced along the way due to the associations you open yourself up to and the ideas you bring back to help grow your business. People in the furniture business are astounded by the added value I continually apply from other industries. It separates me from competitors. It also has put me on the road to making a real difference in the industry by changing the entire way furniture is promoted. I will continue to learn, network, and refine my business because the more value I bring to my customers the more important a resource I become for them.

SEVEN STEPS TO MAKE THE AMERICAN DREAM A REALITY IN YOUR LIFE

Booker T. Washington said, "Excellence is to do something common in an uncommon way." Peak performers operate that way by discovering what they like to do and then doing it well. In the end, this is the only way any of us can ultimately control our own destiny and make the American Dream a reality.

MIKE ROOT is the number one authority on innovative marketing for the home furnishings industry. He has been recognized by the Small Business Administration, the Omaha Chamber of Commerce, and a number of national furniture companies. He is the founder of the Furniture Insider's Club (www.FurnitureInsidersClub.com), a marketing idea factory dedicated to helping retailers sell more with less effort and a lot less cost to the bottom line advertising budget. These ideas help retailers diversify their message and break out of the mold of always advertising "free financing." For marketing ideas applicable to all businesses, not just retail, go to www.FurnitureInsidersClub.com. Mike is the founder of www.GetCustomersRightNow.com, a promotional website to help businesses attract clients, customers and prospects. Mike is also the president of Furniture Sales of Mid-America (www.FurnitureSales.biz), a furniture wholesale company in the Midwest and Rocky Mountain states that has been recognized by numerous national furniture factories for sales excellence. Progressive Furniture, a Sauder company, has twice recognized Furniture Sales as the top sales team and Ligo Products has awarded the top salesman of the year award to Furniture Sales an unprecedented eight out of nine years.

To receive a free copy of his special report "7 Innovative Marketing Strategies to Grow Your Sales by 36.58% in the Next
12 Months" and sign up for a free e-course "Sizzling Hot
Direct Marketing Tips to Make You Money in Any Economy"
go to www.FurnitureInsidersClub.com.

How to Maintain Your Spiritual Life

JOHN KEEL

When many people hear the term "spiritual life," they incorrectly assume or believe it to be synonymous with "religion." Nothing could be further from the truth. To me religion is a man-made system (whether Christianity or any other type of religion), generally accompanied by all sorts of rules about doing this and not doing that. Many "religious" people I know oftentimes act as if they have all the answers, period. And, you're either with them or against them.

One's spiritual life, on the other hand, comes from something internal. For me it comes from my belief in Jesus Christ and is evidenced on the outside by how I live and interact with others. Before you get too excited, understand that I know that many people have a different source of spiritual power – and that's fine. But all of us have something internal; call it a spiritual source that influences us. It gets down to how much attention we pay to it that can make the difference.

Peak performers understand that true success embodies a mix of five areas:

Mental

Emotional

Physical

Financial

Spiritual

I've sometimes seen the five areas diagrammed as spokes on a wheel, with the individual being at the center. And, like any wheel, it turns most efficiently and can gather the most speed if all the spokes are of equal length. Imbalance in any of the five leads to a life that doesn't reach its fullest potential, and in many cases can lead to pain, not just for ourselves but for others.

Why Have a Spiritual Life?

If you had known me twenty years ago, you would have instantly known that my "wheel" was wobbling a lot; although I had enjoyed success in several of the five areas (I was a multimillionaire by the age of 35 and was in great physical shape), my spiritual spoke was almost non-existent. I was under the mistaken impression that spiritual life equaled being religious. And the religion thing wasn't for me.

As with most of us, sometimes it takes a crisis of some kind for us to pay attention. I had mine; it wasn't fun and almost cost me everything I knew to be important to me. Now that I'm "on the other side," I see things more clearly and understand how important the spiritual spoke is to one's overall success, joy, and true peace of mind.

How Do You Make It Real?

The first step I had to take was to understand that my spiritual life wasn't something separate from the rest of my life; it wasn't an activity I did or a way I acted on Sunday. It had to become a part of me, part of my being. In other words, I couldn't act a certain way one day of the week and another way the remaining six; Webster's defines that as hypocrisy. And I'm like everyone else…I didn't want to be known as a hypocrite.

That's the first step: understand that your spiritual life is woven throughout your total life.

The second step was more difficult. I had to change – my thinking, my behavior, my speech, who I hung out with, and so on. It wasn't that I had to do anything; I just didn't want things to be the way they had been. Charlie "Tremendous" Jones once wrote that who you'll be in five years is directly related to what you put in your mind and who you hang out with. And he wasn't just talking about your emotional or financial success.

So I incorporated the process of change. It was several years until I began to see a difference. When we're in the middle of change we don't see what's really occurring, but when people who had known me before commented how I had changed, I knew something was happening. By the way, the change never ends…but you probably already knew that.

What makes our spiritual life different from other types of change, however, is that it's internal first, followed by external later, and the source of the internal change is something outside ourselves. For me, it's something called the Holy Spirit. Step two involves the internal change we implement with the assistance of some higher power.

The third and final step is to "keep on keeping on." That's tied to the ongoing, day-by-day, focus I need to have and implement in growing my spiritual life. And it's really no different from many things – in life we're either growing or dying; there is no middle ground.

For me it doesn't mean perfection; those who know me well, heck, even those who know me only a little, can testify to that. I falter daily, some days worse than others, but it's the knowledge I have that I'm moving in the right direction. As the old song goes, "You pick yourself up, dust yourself off, and start all over again." It is about moving forward on a consistent basis.

How to Maintain Your Spiritual Life

The derivation of maintain is maintenance. I look at maintaining my spiritual life as the maintenance (and growth) of my spiritual life. As with maintaining things that I own, such as my car, there are things I need to do to keep it running, and not just running, but running well.

With my car I change the oil and rotate the tires regularly (my wife, Colleen, would say that this is something I'm actually "religious" about). I also get it washed and cleaned out on somewhat of a regular basis and take it to my car mechanic for regular checkups.

As I'm not an expert on cars, I look to those who are to be able to tell me if there are any foreseeable problems of which I should be aware. It's happened several times that Denny, to whom I've been taking my cars for over 12 years, has pointed out a little situation that if left untouched would turn into a major situation.

So it is with our spiritual lives. There are things we need to do to maintain and grow that part of us.

First is regular implanting outside information in our minds. For me that means regularly reading the Bible (if you have a different spiritual belief there's a "book of knowledge" you want to be regularly reading). It's not just reading that helps me maintain my spiritual engine; I need to be studying it. Just as with the non-spiritual books I read, I highlight and make notes.

Next is a regular time I set aside almost everyday to meditate and pray. To just stop, slow down, and devote time to silence. I was uncomfortable doing this at first (sometimes I still get uncomfortable doing it), but I found that the more regularly I did it, the easier it got. Now I get a little "antsy" if I go more than several days without doing it. Doing it regularly (especially in the morning) gives me an improved perspective on the day.

Developing the habit during this time of giving thanks for all that I've been given, asking about needs that I have, getting myself right (from my thoughts, actions, and words from the previous day) and focusing on other people has helped me to understand that it's not all about me.

The third activity is regular association with a group of people who believe as I do. Yes, for me that's called church. But I've learned that, as with my business life, I can't do it all by myself. Being with others in a group setting on a regular basis helps keep me focused on the things I say and believe are important to me.

Last, it's important to understand that we can't always see things from their true perspective. All of us are good at fooling ourselves. From a spiritual standpoint, I've developed the habit of aligning myself with someone who's further along in the process, someone I respect and trust, and to whom I can be fully accountable. This had led to some significant "external" observations and kept me from what could have been difficult situations.

So there's the key to maintaining your spiritual life: reading, meditating, praying, associating, and finding an accountability partner...all on a consistent basis.

Tying It All Together

Twenty years ago this is the last thing I ever imagined myself doing. As I noted earlier, I had a lot of the trappings of success, but I was missing a critical spoke of the wheel. It was only when I discovered that getting my spiritual life in order could be the missing link that things really changed.

I can summarize "How to Maintain Your Spiritual Life" in several sentences:

1. Understand that if you want to be a true peak performer, you want to have and need an active, growing spiritual life. As I pointed out earlier, that's not about religion.

2. Decide to make your spiritual life an integral part of who and what you are. It's not about something you do on a particular day of the week; it's all about who you become as your spiritual side is intertwined throughout your total life.

3. Work to maintain and grow your spiritual life. It won't be easy; it hasn't been for me, but, from a purely business perspective, the return on investment is the best one you'll find. It has been that way for me; I believe it will that way for you too.

Got questions about this? You can always email with a question. Although I'm excited about the growth we're seeing in my businesses, your and my spiritual life is something about which I really get excited.

JON KEEL has developed an international reputation as a results oriented online business advisor, having been in this arena since January of 1997. In addition to being CEO of Improved Results over a decade ago, he co-developed the Xavier University MBA e-business program, where he taught online marketing and e-commerce for four years. He frequently speaks to audiences about improving the results of their online lead generation and sales channels and has written numerous articles and has appeared on several TV and radio programs. He co-developed the first pay-per-click search engine bid management software and wrote the first book on pay-per-click search engines, "Instant Website Traffic" in 2001. He also contributed to the best selling book, *Success Secrets of the Online Marketing Superstars*. With a master's degree in engineering, Jon moved to Cincinnati in 1971 with the Procter and Gamble Company. He left P&G in 1973 to work for The Henry P. Thompson Company and over a 22-year period became the owner and president/CEO. He sold his interest in the company in 1995 and in 1987 he received an MBA from Xavier University. He lives in the Hyde Park area of Cincinnati with his wife, Colleen.

You can obtain a free copy of a special report, "Using The Internet Effectively" and a CD, "Basics You Need To Know To Shoot Your Website Leads Through The Roof" at www.ImprovedResults.com/PeakPerformers.

From Fear to Faith

ANDRE PALKO

For years, one of the secrets to peak performance was right in front of me every morning, but it didn't reveal itself to me until I was in my forties. I had a few jobs and a few businesses over the years, but nothing really seemed to click.

In my jobs, "success" meant that I'd made it through another work week (well, maybe I had to work Saturday) and that next week I could return to the same place for a paycheck that was usually pretty much the same, maybe with some overtime thrown in. I considered my job to be a fairly good supervisory position, I made decent money, always paid my bills, always had a car and a home. I'm grateful for that, but the nagging feeling that there was something more to this work life gnawed at me.

I was a good performer at work, but there just had to be more. A sense of purpose evaded me and I was definitely not living the life I felt was out there waiting for me. I got my start in the printing industry, and when I had a few years experience and had saved some money, I decided that perhaps I should buy a small printing business.

So in my mid-twenties, with more enthusiasm than common sense and no real business experience to speak of, my effort to buy a small shop in Florida fell through. Instead, some local printers convinced me to open a trade bindery to do finishing and bindery work for printers in the region. Now, if you're a specialist and know what you're doing, this line of work can have some good margins despite a heavy reliance on labor.

My customers were more than happy to give me all the work they didn't care for, but since I was neither a specialist nor experienced, there were no profit margins to speak of. I had just enough knowledge to get into trouble. A little bit of beginner's luck with a couple of good jobs led me to believe this was all going to be okay. Soon however, I was spending far too much on extra labor just to meet commitments and I was scrambling to be all things to too many people. Each month I would anticipate that the next month would be better. I'd simply have to go on the road more, sell more, and work more at night.

The next month would arrive and I'd usually skimp on the sales effort while working more both day and night. About 18 months into this, one of my customers offered me a job managing his small printing company; he said he wanted to semi-retire. I think he simply couldn't bear to watch me struggle anymore. Exhausted, bankrupt but ever hopeful that tomorrow would be better, I took the day job and stayed up half the night trying to keep the business alive. Soon after, I had to throw in the towel. I was back on the dreaded job treadmill.

There was a tiny bit of hope for a buyout at the print shop, and that motivated me for a while, but the owner was wisely unwilling to fund more risky growth with his retirement money. I was negative in the funds department and desperately needed a better paying job. My old friend and original employer made a timely and attractive offer at just the right time. So, it was back to my original job supervising a bindery department for a mid-size printing company.

For ten years I stayed with that job for fear I wouldn't be able to replace the income and benefits if I got into another business or looked for a better job. Maybe tomorrow I would work on that; there was too much to do today. Well, tomorrow came in the form of downsizing when the company lost its largest single account. I was fortunate and got offered a job right away, but it only lasted about one year until 9-11 and the downsizing that followed.

I was demoralized, and working the graveyard shift doing menial jobs at another printing company to make ends meet didn't help matters. In hindsight, I think it took all that to get me to pay attention to what God was saying to me.

Sharing my complaints with a friend one night, he asked me, "So what can you do about it today?" That's when it clicked for me. This day is all I have to work with. I may not be here tomorrow and what happened yesterday can't be changed. So focus on today.

It was a moment of liberation that changed everything. For me, the secret to peak performance started with the simple act of keeping it in the day. Every morning I was opening my eyes to the day before me, but I had always been too busy to see it for the gift that it is, or I was so anxious about what tomorrow might bring I let today slide away unfulfilled. Here was peace, freedom and utter simplicity. Here's how it works.

First, since all I have is today, I better make it good. I make a simple plan the night before and prioritize. In those early days, this was a matter of going to work at night, then spending the day split between job hunting, working on a part-time equipment business (I was persistent if nothing else), and looking for other business opportunities. This planning and prioritizing continues to evolve with my education in the business world, but I always try to keep it as simple as possible. Today I ask: "Is this a money-making task and if not, can I delegate it?"

Second, I make a point at the end of each day to be grateful for the blessings of the day. Even on the most difficult days, there is much to remember in gratitude. Not once in my life have I gone without food, clothing, or shelter. Problems usually turn out to be opportunities in disguise. For instance, had I not lost my job, I would never have found the opportunity that grew into today's successful business. An attitude of gratitude is critical.

Important, too, in my daily plan is to remember that I am a physical, mental, and spiritual being. So I schedule activities that are important to my health such as exercise; I see a trainer three times a week. I schedule time for daily Catholic mass and volunteer activities. And, I remember to schedule time for fun stuff as well although I admit I probably need a bit of work in that department. These are all just as important to me as the scheduling of my daily business. Of course as a human being, I am a constant work in progress...just ask my wife.

There are four things I do to reinforce my practice.

1. I never stop learning. Every book, seminar, business coach, and CD or DVD course is an investment that helps me to make each day more productive. In my old way of thinking, I felt I couldn't afford to spend this kind of money. Today, I know I can't afford not to invest. Every investment like this has had something positive to take away from it and has at the very least, paid for itself.

2. I stick with positive, like-minded people and at all costs avoid negative, complaining, doom and gloom types. They are toxic.

3. I persist. Every "no" brings me one step closer to a "yes." There is value in failure as long as I persist in moving forward and look to learn from my mistakes. All my experience in those jobs is now a major asset in my business. If I didn't have that experience, I never would have recognized the fantastic opportunity that turned into my core business. I've learned that my customers will gladly pay to learn from my mistakes and my experience – who would have known! Trust me, you don't want to give up before the miracle happens.

4. I give away at least 10% of what I earn. Why? The popular mindset is that the world is a zero-sum game, in other words, if one person is making money, another must be losing, that there's only so much to go around. To succeed, we must shed this false and dangerous belief because it is based on fear. The truth is that wealth is infinite, with enough to go around for everyone on earth that is willing and able to work for it.

Fear will isolate you from the limitless opportunities that surround you. Fear is reactive rather than proactive; it puts you in a defensive position that lets others determine what's best for you. And they do not have your best interests in mind!

To succeed, we need to move from fear to faith. Faith that God will, indeed, provide. Faith that there is a position of value for you in the world and, that once you find it, you will be rewarded. Faith that if you make a mistake, there can be good to come of it. Giving 10% requires a huge leap of faith, especially when you don't have a lot of money. I know because I began this practice when I was in huge debt and felt like I couldn't afford to do such a thing, but I took that leap and ever since, I have never lacked for anything.

Ironically, it seems that the more we give the more we receive. It's not about the money, it's about fundamentally changing the way you live your life. I've lost the old fear-based way of life and I can say with absolute confidence that this practice will change the way you live for the better. Once you take that giant leap, you will never look backwards or forwards in fear, and you will know a freedom and serenity not otherwise possible.

Today you should congratulate yourself. Reading this book puts you in a select 20%. According to Bookpublishing.com, 80% of US families did not buy or read a book last year, and 58% of adults never read a book after high school! This simple act of reading gives you a giant head start in making the most of today.

ANDRE PALKO was bitten by the entrepreneurial bug at the age of 12 when he began selling flower seeds and delivering grocery store flyers door-to-door in his hometown of Frederick, Maryland. His introduction to the printing industry came while he was playing bass guitar for a New York City rock and roll band in 1980. The band's lead singer was part of a family printing business and it wasn't long before Andre was packing boxes and learning a trade by day, while taking classes at Columbia University and playing clubs by night. Today, he is president of Technifold USA with his wife and business partner, Gina. Their company provides patented solutions and unique strategies that enable printers to get up to twice their normal yield from bindery and finishing equipment. Customers include the top printing companies and finishing equipment manufacturers in the world.

For fun he pilots a Cessna 172 aircraft and has moved from the likes of New York clubs like the famed CBGB's to the church hall, playing bass and singing with a contemporary choir throughout New Jersey. His daughter Meghan is a junior at UNC Wilmington.

For a Free subscription to Technifold's Bindery Success™ newsletter plus a Free download of their 15-Part Bindery How-To Course, go to www.technifoldusa.com/peak.html You'll get valuable hands-on tips and tricks that your bindery and finishing department can start using today to instantly improve production.

Master the Art of Business Self-Defense™

RON ROSENBERG & LORIE ROSENBERG

"How to kick butt, crush the competition, and make more money in less time than you ever dreamed possible!"

You wouldn't think of walking down a city street at night without being aware, alert, and prepared. And yet, even as you read this, your business is vulnerable to attack – at any time – from ruthless competitors, government regulations, and an unpredictable economy.

But it doesn't have to be this way. In this chapter, marketing and customer service expert Ron Rosenberg and his business partner Lorie Rosenberg will share ten proven marketing and business tactics to help you defend your business and outmaneuver your competition. It's a must read!

If you're like most small businesses today, you've been plugging along steadily, even in times like these when customers are more demanding and more cost conscious than ever. But you simply *want more*. Actually you *need more* to cover your increased labor costs, insurance, supplies, and other expenses that are making it increasingly difficult to run your business, much less make a profit.

The good news is that even in a bad economy, you can <u>dramatically</u> grow your business and increase your income...you just have to know how. Because there *are* businesses that understand how to weather these downward trends and use outrageous marketing strategies to get people to take action –even when money is tight.

But first you need to develop a winning mindset, to know that you can succeed even when times are tough and the odds are stacked against you. And you do this by learning from people who've "been there and done that." From mentors, experts, and coaches, who've paved the way with time-tested, proven, and innovative marketing techniques that *consistently deliver results.*

Take the martial arts for example. Your "sensei" or teacher guides you through the ranks to help you achieve your black belt. But it takes a lot of hard work and dedication. Imagine the way you'd feel once you passed your grueling, physically demanding, two-hour black belt testing...

As you stand proudly in front of your family and friends who've just witnessed your incredible performance, the head instructor presents you with a neatly folded black belt and shakes your hand as he congratulates you on your promotion. You proceed to tie your black belt around your waist in the traditional martial arts style and all of your friends and loved ones in the audience clap their hands, scream their approval, and take your picture. Wow! You've just achieved a goal that's taken a lot of dedicated work and effort and you're completely speechless, except for that amazing grin on your face and the joy bursting from your belly.

Isn't that exactly what you want to experience in your own business? Knowing that you have mastered the type of advanced marketing techniques that can help you beat the competition and put more money in your pocket in less time than you ever thought possible?

Well you can *and you will*, but there are <u>ten skills and behaviors</u> you need to master to create an endless stream of loyal customers, to defend against encroaching competition, and to create a thriving, sustainable, kick-butt business:

1. Attentive – When you're attacked, whether it's a physical assault on the street or from a competitor down the block, you always need to be aware of your environment and your surroundings. You see, you never know when or where an attack might come from. You basically need eyes in the back of your head to sense the warning signs so you can avoid an attack in the first place. By understanding your organization and being attentive to your business environment, you will always have a defensive counter strategy to ward off any type of assault.

2. Defensive – As a business person, it shouldn't be your desire to attack your competitors and try to put them out of business. There usually is enough business for everyone. However, it's important to defend your competitive position to continue to grow and be successful. That's why you must understand all the weapons available in your arsenal to defend your business and not be outmaneuvered or outperformed by a competitor. It's the same on the street. You should feel confident in all the

options you have to protect yourself and feel safe and secure wherever you go.

3. Disciplined – This is one of the most critical areas that will determine whether you're successful or not in your business and in your life. That's because it takes discipline to train for any possible problem that might arise. You need to maintain a strict schedule of workouts to ensure that you're physically fit. And you should do the same thing in your business to stay "fiscally fit." Business Self-Defense™ is not for slackers...it's for people who have the discipline to train hard and become successful.

4. Decisive – This is no time for the faint of heart. With the competitive nature of today's business environment, companies need to take decisive steps to counter the aggressive tactics of their competitors. By selecting a definitive course of action based on knowledge and experience, and carrying it through without hesitation or deviation, businesses, as well as individuals, can survive a direct attack and come out, perhaps a little cut and bruised, but definitely on the winning end of the battle.

5. Aggressive – Small businesses and associations should develop unique skills to survive in today's competitive world. It's not uncommon for a big-box company to move in down the street and completely destroy a company that's been in business for years. That's why you need to use all of the resources at your disposal and use them ruthlessly to survive assaults from multiple attackers and from a variety of directions. When you're out-numbered, you must do whatever is necessary to counter your attacks to save your life and your business. Use every strategy

you can to distinguish yourself from the competition and create a reason for prospects to choose you over your competition.

6. Speedy – The perfect fight is the one that is over before the opponent understands what hit him. And that can be a big problem today...you may not even be aware that an attack is coming and once you do, it may be too late. That's why you always have to be aware of your environment so you can adapt to new trends, changing technologies, and fickle prospects. Once you see that a change needs to be made, you can move quickly before your competitor overtakes you. In many situations, speed is power and that's what you need to survive.

7. Confident – As with any confrontation, whether it's on the street or in a boardroom, you need to always maintain a confident frontal defense. Your competition can sense weakness in your business, from how you hire employees to the way you treat your customers. If they see an opening where they can steal some of your business and cut in on your profits, they won't hesitate to do so. That's why you should work hard to maintain a strong following of customers who want to do business with you. By positioning yourself as a confident, profitable enterprise, you'll scare away ruthless competitors who will do anything to try to hone in on your territory and ambush your business.

8. Focused – Your ability to focus on a task is one of the most important qualities you can have to be successful. Because when you put all of your energy towards achieving a single goal, it usually gets accomplished. When you continually stray from a task or get distracted, you never seem to accomplish anything. Sometimes giving yourself a hard deadline kicks you into high

gear and helps you move forward faster. You'll be amazed at your progress and you'll be proud of your accomplishment.

9. Unexpected – In any competitive environment, you should be prepared for the unexpected. Most businesses copy what others are doing in their industry and hope they do it better. What they don't understand is that most times it's better to try something unusual and unexpected and completely differentiate themselves from the competition. That's your Unique Selling Proposition and it can truly set you apart. By doing what your competition least expects, you take them out of the match entirely. And your customers will love you for it!

10. Successful – To be successful, you need to win before the battle even begins. You always have to be on the lookout for new ideas and strategies from mentors and coaches, from books and learning resources, and from studying what others are doing successfully in your industry and in other industries. When you work on your business; when you work with people who have a track record; when you differentiate yourself from your competition; and when you move quickly and decisively on your goals, there's no way you can lose. It's a proven formula for success.

By incorporating these 10 tactics into your business arsenal, you'll be on your way to becoming a true practitioner of the Business Self-Defense™ philosophy. Not everyone can achieve a "black belt" in a traditional martial arts program, but you *can* become certified as a **Black Belt** in **Business Self-Defense™**. You can learn the strategies and techniques we teach to achieve wealth and security in your business and you can receive your own authentic "black belt" (embroidered with your name) in Business Self-Defense™.

In our unique program, you'll learn specific business self-defense tactics you can use to significantly increase your business, whether you're attracting new customers or adding new types of revenue. Plus, you'll be able to talk with us one-on-one and get expert advice on specific questions about your business. Where else can you get this type of broad knowledge from people who have learned from the best and are willing to share this valuable knowledge with you?

Most people are awed by those of us who have earned their black belt. Now, you too can earn a black belt in an area that's important to your success: *your business.* Our simple step-by-step approach will guide you through the process, helping you apply what you've learned immediately to your own business and helping you reap the rewards of improved business results. It takes motivation, integrity, and focus to become a Black Belt in Business Self-Defense™. Once you do, you'll see how this knowledge will help you grow your business more in the next year than you've done in the last *several* years. It's a winning proposition...one that will separate you from your competition and set the stage for continued success in the future.

Ron Rosenberg

Master of Business Self-Defense,

Tactical Instructor, Speaker, and Head Coach

Ron Rosenberg is a nationally recognized and award-winning expert on marketing, customer service, and business improvement. He's a 5th degree black belt with over 25 years experience teaching, performing, and competing in Isshin-Ryu and Sanshinkai Karate.

With this diverse background, Ron shows individuals how to accomplish goals they only dreamed possible by helping them access the resources at their disposal – both internal and external. People who complete his Business Self-Defense™ program gain the skills, motivation and belief system they need to succeed in their businesses!

Lorie Rosenberg

Master of Business Self-Defense,

Mindset Instructor and Women's Self-Defense Coach

Lorie Rosenberg has worked in the field of marketing and communications for over 30 years as an advertising account executive, copywriter, and graphic artist. She has 1st degree black belts in both Isshin-Ryu and Sanshinkai Karate, and has taught women's self-defense programs.

With her experience in the spiritual component of the martial arts – overcoming overwhelming obstacles and mental and physical barriers – Lorie is uniquely qualified to help individuals overcome their own limiting beliefs and gain the discipline and motivation to achieve personal growth and business success.

To sign up for our FREE webinar, "Cracking the Secret Code to Business Self-Defense™," with 7 specific strategies to "kick butt" in your business and make more money now, go to www.BusinessSelf-Defense.com/peak or contact us at 800-260-0662 or e-mail us at info@qualitytalk.com.

How an Introvert with a Poor Self Image Raised Himself from Failure to Success and Earned the Right to be Counted Among the Elite Financial and Estate Planning Advisors: The Missteps and Mistakes that Almost Completely Derailed His Success with the Affluent

SCOTT KEFFER

Imagine Charlie Brown trying to sell millionaires.

That was me; an introvert with a poor self image fighting every step of the way against his inborn fear of rejection to learn the secrets of marketing and advising the affluent. It was a journey that took a huge investment of time, energy, and money, but has paid off financially and personally resulting in a level of satisfaction and respect among my clients and peers that has exceeded anything I could have ever imagined. The missteps and mistakes I made along the way could fill a book (in fact they have). More times than I care to count, I thought of giving up, changing careers, doing anything but continuing to endure the rejection and frustration.

If you're new to the world of financial services and estate planning or if you're discouraged from beating your head against the wall, you may not feel you have the time or the energy to go through what I did to reach success. You want to get there faster. I don't blame you. I get it and I'm on a mission to help you get there faster, with less pain, and less money.

Why? I love helping my clients disinherit the IRS in favor of their family and charity and I've found that I get even more energy mentoring and coaching other advisors. I want you to know the satisfaction and the financial rewards that come from helping the affluent achieve their dreams. That's why I'm sharing the storehouse of knowledge and strategies that I've gained from trial and error and by learning from the best authorities on marketing, branding, and selling, so you can take years off your trajectory. At the end of this chapter you'll find a free offer for a special report on the 25 biggest mistakes I made on the way to achieving success with high net worth clients. I want you to know the mistakes, so you can avoid them without having to burn your own hand.

But first, a bit about where I came from, see if any of this sounds familiar. It was a bitter cold, windy day, like many winter days are north of Chicago, and a chubby, shy nine-year-old stood plastered against the side of the school building during recess desperately afraid of introducing himself to someone new. And when class resumed, it got worse: I was asked to stand and introduce myself. I would have rather died. I really thought I was going to lose my lunch.

Later, I would find out why meeting new people and speaking in front of people was so painful. I'm an introvert. It's not that I don't like people, I do. It's just that they take energy. Some people gain energy when they interact with people; introverts, like me, lose energy. Could an introvert like me really become successful advising high net worth clients?

As a teenager, I dreamed of owning my own business. It was this promise that would later entice me to give up my corporate job to be my own boss and have "unlimited" potential in the life insurance business. After five years of mediocrity, I realized I couldn't sell and escaped to the wholesale side of the financial services industry.

After a decade in the wholesale side supporting elite estate and financial advisors, the dream of building my own estate planning firm tailored exclusively to the affluent enticed me back into the retail side of the planning business. I wanted to work exclusively with the affluent (who doesn't?). One huge problem: I was still an introvert with a recovering self-image and I had no affluent clients. In fact, I had no clients at all.

A few years after I borrowed the money to start my own business, when that money was starting to run out with next to nothing coming in, I got serious and wrote down a set of goals, dreams really. To be considered one of the elite practitioners in the financial services and estate-planning arena, I figured I had to start by earning membership in The International Forum; then I wanted to teach my Forum colleagues in a workshop at their national conference; and, finally, I wanted to speak from the main platform. Those are just three of the 101 things that I wrote down that day.

Well, I've already accomplished two of those three goals. It's hard to describe how I felt when I was accepted for membership in the forum; it's even harder to describe how I felt when I was chosen to present a workshop to colleagues. I knew I'd come a very long way from those dim days standing in front of the class.

Today I have earned the trust of nearly 100 very wealthy families who have taken my advice to preserve their wealth for future generations and leave a charitable legacy, and I have mentored hundreds of advisers around North America, sharing the special skills and strategies that won me success in my business. All of those advisers, including Salvadore R. Salvo of Summit Financial Resources, Inc., in Parsippany, New Jersey, have achieved significant revenue and bottom line growth in their practices.

It's hugely gratifying to receive comments like this:

"My revenue has increased by 73%!" says Salvo. "Scott Keffer is one of the most talented professionals I have ever met. He and his advice have been a godsend to me and my team."

Robert Wright, JD, estate-planning attorney in Fresno, California says, "I have watched Scott mature over the last 15 years into an expert on marketing, branding, and motivating others to take action – his expertise in this area is clearly special. He has positively impacted my bottom line, returning in excess of 10 times my investment with him."

"Scott is one of the best marketing minds I know, not to mention a top notch estate and financial planner. He is the real deal – not pie-in-the-sky theory, but proven tools, ideas, systems, and processes that produce incredible amounts of revenue," adds Randy Fox, CFP, founding principle of InKnowVision, a strategic outsource to advisors of the ultra-wealthy.

One of the first things I show advisers who want to succeed the way I have is my list of the 25 biggest mistakes. Mistakes I made trying to gain high net worth clients. Mistakes that cost me hundreds of thousands of dollars in lost business and almost derailed my journey! Mistakes like:

- Choosing the wrong time (and the wrong person) to establish your credibility with a wealthy prospect – and why making this classic blunder virtually dooms your efforts to close successfully.

- Giving into the temptation to play the super hero and why no matter how good it feels, it's bad for you, bad for your client, and disastrous for your bottom line.

- Forgetting (or never having been taught) the powerful technique that history's most influential teachers and philosophers have used to increase influence – and how using it can boost your credibility through the roof – and how not using it may be the very reason you are not more successful with the affluent.

If you'd like to learn more about these and the 22 other mistakes to avoid, see the free offer at the end of the chapter.

The road from failure to success has had its bumps and potholes and an abundance of hard earned lessons that apply to every business. These lessons can never be taken away from me. I've paid for every one of them. Now they allow me to face an always uncertain future with more confidence and hope. I'd like to share them briefly with you.

- **Written Goals** – Inside my day planner, I carry my dog-eared list – what I call my Success 101 goals – which I wrote out in 1997, soon after I opened my business. It took me six years to qualify for the forum, a minimum of a half million dollars of revenue, and fourteen years to teach a workshop and I have yet to speak from the main platform, but I will. What's next for you?

- **Learning from Failure** – What a waste to go through the pain and agony of failure and not gain from it. Yet, that's what I was doing. Dan Sullivan, one of my long-term coaches, shared the value of learning from mistakes. Do you have a process to "mine the gold" from every mistake?

- **Acting Against Fear** – There aren't many days that I still don't wake up thinking, *What can go wrong today?* One of my consultants (and I've had many), whom I admired for his courage, gave me real clarity about courage. He told me that courage is acting against fear, and since he didn't have any fear, he couldn't be regarded as courageous. His admiration of my courage continues to inspire me. What are you afraid of today?

- **Mentors** – I have ridden with Winston Churchill, Abraham Lincoln, Jesus Christ, and many other heroes that mentor me daily through CDs and books. Charlie "Tremendous" Jones, the well-known author, said, "You will be tomorrow what you are today, except for the people you meet and the books you read." Who are you riding with tomorrow?

- **Coaching** – Tiger Woods still has a coach. Think about that. Tiger Woods, one of the greatest golfers of all time, is taking constructive feedback from a golfer he could crush in competition! Why would Tiger still have a coach at his elite level? Who's your next coach?

- **Investing in Personal Growth** – Where can you spend $50,000 and get a guaranteed 100 percent rate of return: new house, cars, toys, or the stock market? An investment in yourself – in your knowledge, skills, and capabilities – will return 100 fold or more and the value will be with you year after year. Long ago, I made the decision to invest at least 10 percent of my time and income every year in personal development. What's your personal growth budget?

- **Strengthen Your Strengths** – "Work on your weaknesses" was the conventional wisdom drilled into me from my youth. Then one day, Dan Sullivan challenged me to consider the outcome of a life spent strengthening weaknesses – mediocrity. There's much more to be gained with a laser focus on strengthening your strengths. Do you have a Strengthen My Strengths Plan?

- **Lifetime Learning** – "Stop learning and start dying" is one of my mantras. Bill Gates, the world's third richest man said, "I also place a high value on having a passion for ongoing learning." Do you have a Top Ten to Be Learned List?

- **Mastery** – Mastery is about the power of sustained improvement. Relentlessly moving in one direction, step by step, day by day and then one day, bang – skyrocketing improvement. What are you applying the Five Core Principles of Mastery to?

- **Living with Purpose** – Finally, and most importantly, it was about discovering my role on the planet. The purpose for my existence. To find the answer, I went to the source: my Creator. I found the answer in His blueprint, the Bible. Through the process of seeking to discover my purpose, I met my Creator through a personal relationship with Jesus

Christ, who has transformed me and continues to transform me by leading me day by day to live out my purpose and forgiving me when I fall short. Have you found your Purpose on the Planet?

Written goals, learning from failure, acting against fear, mentors, coaching, investing in personal growth, strengthening your strengths, a commitment to lifetime learning, mastery and living with purpose, plus some special skills and capabilities have all helped this Charlie Brown raise himself from failure to success. You can too!

SCOTT KEFFER is a nationally recognized financial educator, speaker, advisor, and mentor to financial advisors and estate planning attorneys across the United States and Canada. As an expert in wealth preservation, he has been interviewed on radio and TV and has conducted presentations to over fourteen thousand individuals. In his role as a continuing education instructor, Scott has instructed thousands of attorneys, accountants, and other financial advisors. His articles have appeared in *Physician's News Digest, Resort Living, National Underwriter, Dynamic Business* and other publications. He has advised wealthy individuals and families from coast to coast for three decades. His counsel and assistance have saved them over $712 million in estate, income, and capital gains taxes. He is the past president of the National Association of Family Wealth Counselors, a member of many professional organizations including The International Forum, AALU, National Committee on Planned Giving, and the Estate Planning Council.

Scott is the innovative creator of Legacy Planning®, along with The Legacy Planning® Process, The Donor Motivation Program™, The Donor Motivation Advisor Network, The Elite Advisor Edge™, The Affluent Engagement System™ among others. He lives in Pittsburgh, Pennsylvania with his wife and children and their chocolate lab.

To get your FREE copy of Scott Keffer's special report, "The 25 Biggest Mistakes I Made Trying to Work with the Affluent and What I Learned to Get Them to Practically Beg Me to Do Business With Them," go to www.eliteadvisoredge.com and look for the special limited time offer.

Innovation and Change

ROBERT PHELAN

A Model for Innovation

'We can't solve the world's problems by using the same kind of thinking we used when we created them."

—Albert Einstein

Innovation has become a prerequisite for success in today's rapid-fire world. What do you see when you walk the aisles of any retail store? What do you see when you visit the website Amazon.com? What do you see on the social networks and Internet and blogosphere? Everything is new. Not new this year or new this week or new this month but in many cases new today or new this minute. Innovation is everywhere and every peak performer has to be part of it.

It's easy to think of innovation as someone else's problem like those who have it in their job description as CEO or the new CIO, not Chief Information Officer but Chief Innovation Officer or the R&D department. Whether you are a solo entrepreneur, own a company or work for someone else, in this article I am going to ask you to apply a much broader definition to innovation. If you are a peak performer and want to remain in that special class, you first have to innovate you and how you view the world.

Consider some of these statistics taken from a popular YouTube video called "Did you know":

- There are over 200 million registered users on MySpace. There are 230,000 new users on MySpace every day. If MySpace were a country, it would be the 5th largest in the world (between Indonesia and Brazil).

- In July of 2008, Google hosted 235 million searches per day.

- Eight billion text messages are sent and received per day.

- The number of Internet devices in 1992 was one million. In 2008 it's one billion.

- It is estimated that 4 exabytes (4.1 x 10 18th) of unique information will be generated this year. A popular expression claims that "all words ever spoken by human beings" could be stored in approximately 5 exabytes of data. (Let that sink in – there are six billion people on the planet today.)

- By 2013 a supercomputer will be built that exceeds the computational capabilities of the human brain. Predictions are that by 2049, a $1000 computer will exceed the computational capabilities of the entire human species.

You can ride the innovation tsunami or get swept away by it. Make a choice today to sit on top of this wave and take a long ride with it into the future.

I believe you can become an expert innovator with a simple approach I call "Model and Change." As the management guru Peter F. Drucker said in his book *Innovation and Entrepreneurship*, innovation is rarely sparked by a "flash of genius," but is more often the product of "organized, systematic, rational work." Ray Kroc, the founder of McDonalds did not invent the hamburger but saw how the drive-in concept could be simplified, standardized, and multiplied. Likewise Howard Schultz, founder of Starbucks, didn't invent the coffee shop but saw an opportunity to make the coffee shop experience special and he did it on a worldwide scale. Michael Dell didn't invent the PC but he decided to make every PC to order and sell directly to the customer without a middleman. He's now #11 on the Forbes 400 and worth $17.3 billion. Not a bad ROI for a modest innovation.

Here's my simple three-step formula to help you think like a great innovator:

1. **Look through the lens of innovation.** From now on, whatever you see or hear or experience, ask yourself how is this different from before and figure out what was changed. Two great examples today are the Amazon Kindle electronic book reader and Barack Obama's presidential campaign. The Kindle didn't reinvent the book. It just puts the book in digital form. Amazon didn't invent the digital book idea either. They "modeled and changed' what Sony had already invented. President Obama didn't rely on big donors to fund his campaign. Instead he went to the Internet and used modern technology to acquire many smaller donors and set records in fundraising. To become an innovator you need to think like an innovator and the best

way to build this skill is through assiduous observation of what others are doing.

2. **Model what you see.** Take what you see and model it for your purposes. Here's a business example. I sell products and services to middle market companies. Looking through the lens of innovation, I began to notice that many cutting edge ideas launched by the companies selling my type products/ services to the Fortune 500 eventually migrated down market in a simplified form. Once I identified this trend, I changed my company mission statement to, "providing Fortune 500-type products and services to the middle market." I then either created similar products/services; searched for companies that would bring those F500 ideas to the middle market; worked with them to adapt the ideas to the middle market; licensed the ideas and made them available to the middle market; or created joint ventures with partners who could bring a service to the middle market.

3. **Change and improve.** The next part of the formula is to tweak it in some way to make it better than the original. We see this in consumer products all the time with what the marketing folks call a line extension, i.e. Budweiser to Bud Light or Oreo cookies with the original filling to Oreos with twice the filling. The possibilities are endless. When you start to look through the lens of innovation, you wonder what took them so long to create these variations. I've learned the hard way that all change must be constant and never ending. Sometimes we think we have such a great idea that no one can copy it. Wrong! It's just a matter of how fast and how much better their version will be. As

dominant and even monopolistic a position as Microsoft has, Google is investing a big pile of cash to convert everyone to web-hosted software as an alternative. And somewhere in California or Mumbai or Beijing, there is a young team of innovators who are planning the downfall of Google. As economist Joseph Schumpeter described the "creative destruction of capitalism," none of us are safe from innovation.

4. **Bonus Step.** Master entrepreneur and business consultant Eben Pagan says that you have to position the mind of the prospect, not position your product or service. When you are innovating, you want to do your best to get out of an existing brain bucket. Think of car rental companies. You can probably think of six or seven and that's about all. Instead of tweaking the car rental model and becoming number eight where you'll either be forgotten or have no impact on the market, it's better to create a whole new model and be number one. In the car rental category check out zipcar.com, they are number one in a category where you can rent by the hour instead of by the day or the week. Google "hourly car rental" and see what comes up first. Model and change to a new category and you'll own your market.

In order to innovate your business you need to innovate yourself. You can't be a source of change unless you change who you are. What is the skill set of the people in the space where you want to be a peak performer? What is their knowledge? Who are your friends and associates? Are they innovators or are they hanging on to the models of the past? Who are in your social networks? Are you and your company at the bleeding edge or the dying edge?

Read and study. Study and read. Peak performers are insatiable learners. Our digital world makes learning easy. You can download over 190,000 titles to an Amazon Kindle in less than a minute and carry them with you wherever you go. Every course imaginable is available via home study, CD, DVD, online, podcast or other digital media.

Innovators learn and pay attention to everything. Then, when they time is right, they have a moment of inspiration and change the world for all of us. Be an innovator and change the world forever.

Robert Phelan is a thirty-year veteran of the insurance industry. Having worked for major brokerage firms throughout New England, Bob is currently Chairman and CEO of Litchfield Insurance Group. In his capacity as CEO, Bob has led his company to national prominence in providing a wide range of value-added services to its clients. Litchfield was named by *Rough Notes Magazine*, the largest circulation trade journal dedicated to the insurance brokerage business, as Marketing Agency of the Month for May 2001 and then received the ultimate recognition of Agency of the Year 2001 by the same publication. Bob has a bachelor's from Tufts University, holds the professional designation of Associate in Risk Management as well as Certified WorkComp Advisor. In addition, he is a distinguished graduate of The Buckley School of Public Speaking. In January 2005, after conducting a nationwide search, The National Alliance Research Academy recognized Mr. Phelan as one of "The 25 Most Innovative Agents in America." The profiles of all 25 were published in a book by the same name. He is a member of the Editorial Advisory Board of *Rough Notes Magazine* and has spoken throughout the U.S. and Canada on the topic, "Differentiation through Value-Added Services."

How to Capitalize on Change

MARK JACKSON

O ne certainty in life is that times must and always do change. Okay, you have probably heard this one before. Mostly likely you have heard the phrase on more than one occasion. The statement may even make sense to you, but how do you handle the reality of its truth? And better yet, if you believe change is always coming how can you possibly be ready to take advantage of that impending change? Good questions, huh? We'll come back to them.

Back in the mid 90s, I was an operations accountant for a large transportation company. My personal life and career were moving along just fine. Then our main competitor had a labor strike. The impact of that strike, while lasting less than two weeks brought on great change for my firm and me.

Imagine working in a climate-controlled, well-furnished office environment everyday, lunch breaks, expense account, 401k and stock purchase plans, the whole nine yards. These are the trappings of your day-to-day life. Then without notice you are told to pick up a pair of work boots, a handheld package scanner and have a map book thrust into your hands. You're given the keys to a truck only a long haul driver could love and a driver from the local temporary work force earning $8.50 per hour.

Then, if this were not enough, you are sent out to deliver over 500 packages to 75 different businesses. You have a maximum of 10 hours to complete this task with a 45-minute commute to and from the delivery route. Imagine you experience all this with no promise of ever seeing your cushy desk job again. We are talking about going from paradise to the desert, steak to spam, champagne to beer.

In the midst of this experience, I was also buying my first home. At the closing table I had the opportunity to review a multi-page document on legal paper. It had within it a few pages containing digital images right on the page. Pictures taken with a digital camera for which I truly only needed a good excuse to go buy at the time.

Additionally, the document made good use of a database software program moving core information through out multiple legal sized pages. Lastly, there were a few pages that presented ratios, depreciation schedules and other mathematic calculations. With a background in accounting and computer information systems, I had an epiphany. I looked at my wife and said, "I don't know what this it, but I could do it." My realtor expressed I was holding the real estate appraisal.

Now what was a guy who was one day sitting at his desk, the next riding in a dusty van with Goober doing thinking about becoming an real estate appraiser? You got it, experiencing change.

Fast-forward three years. Okay, I admit it; it took that long for me to realize I wasn't going back to my cushy desk job. The days of lunch breaks and A/C were long gone, but fortunately for me not the possibility to capitalize on being an appraiser. So it was off to school to get licensed and become an entrepreneur. The motivation to get my butt in gear had been compounded by more than the desk job not coming back. The physical demands were showing in my body along with a growing disdain for a management team lacking definite direction.

Now this is where my decision to make changes began producing real capital. In less than two years I was blessed to open my own real estate appraisal firm with six other appraisers working for me. Interest rates were low and property values were soaring while new construction was everywhere.

Seeing more people getting right sized after the tragedy of 9/11 and wanting to become appraisers, I opened a school to train them in the practical aspects of the profession. Before long, I sold the appraisal business for a great profit, but kept the school, which was a cash cow with little overhead. Why, because with interest rising rates in the mid 2000s and less purchase and refinance mortgage business, the amount of appraisal work available was slowing. It just so happened the number of people who wanted to be appraisers was not waning. My ability to see change and capitalize on it was becoming greatly enhanced.

With no appraisals to do, but a changing real estate market, the time was ripe to start buying residential property. However, as an appraiser with an understanding of how to analyze valuation trends and neighborhood markets I had a unique advantage over the typical real estate investor.

With a good measure of immediate success, other real estate investors began asking how I was able to locate and value deals while avoiding the pitfalls of declining property values. With that InvestorCompsOnline. com was born. InvestorCompsOnline.com is an Internet resource real estate investors and others nationwide could go to and get meaningful valuation training and data. Actually, InvestorCompsOnline.com is like having your own personal real estate appraiser riding with you everywhere you go.

You see, once again, a change in the market arena was met with an opportunity to capitalize on that change. So we are back to "times must and always do change." The primary focus here is what are you going to do when change comes *your* way? Sink or swim? Capitalize or crumble?

I can tell you there was one further change taking place that I had no idea of how to capitalize on or that the arena even existed – the world of direct marketing and building a true info-marketing business. It wasn't until I was invited to attend the Renegade Million event held in Cleveland, Ohio with Dan Kennedy and Bill Glazer did I see another change to capitalize on coming.

There, Bill Glazer and Lee Milteer introduced the newly founded Peak Performers Group. This is a gathering of individuals, with a broad spectrum of businesses and interests, who would be exposed to Lee's teaching on time management, goal setting, and personal growth. Furthermore, Bill brought to full bare the mass of his tactics and skills for creating emotion driven copy and marketing campaigns to sell effectively.

It is through this group and its associations of roughly 75-100 business principles that I was able to grow my business to new levels. Peak performers stimulates creativity while promoting accountability and focus to execute plans. With this strategic impetus, I have been continually able to capitalize through the ongoing changes in the real estate and financial markets.

There is one component of managing change and potentially capitalizing on it. That is knowing whether the changes, which are occurring around you, mean you should stand still or get moving. There are times when making the decision to leap at an opportunity because it appears appealing will be challenging. Internally, it will take self-examination of the logic or emotion tingling inside you.

One of the phrases Lee Milteer uses is being aware of the "bright shiny objects" which may look like an opportunity or pending change in direction. The fact is, as action-minded entrepreneurs, those bright shiny objects are merely distractions being placed before you for other-worldly or less than holistic reasons. Distractions get you off track, off purpose. Identify and beware of bright shiny objects. Stay focused on your core goals.

As you go through your personal and professional career, when you see change coming that requires you to move, THEN BY GOD MOVE. One of the greatest pieces of wisdom I can share with you is to take action and implement. Nothing is going to happen by wishing it so. Get to it.

If you want to be home to raise your children, begin a non-profit to serve your community, write books which speak of the wisdom gleaned from your childhood and developmental years, or learn to play piano to share the gift of music with others, or all of these, then get to it. Whatever is your desire, get to it.

You don't have to become an appraiser, and you don't have to face the challenge of becoming one as the result of an epiphany. But you should constantly push yourself to improve at whatever it is you do. Learn something new daily. I constantly hear about people claiming to have

20 years of experience, when all they actually have is the same one-year of experience repeated 20 times.

Make sure you're learning, implementing, and challenging yourself to reach new levels – doesn't matter if it's physical or mental exercise – I can promise you will never capitalize on any change standing still. Get to it.

MARK JACKSON has written over a hundred articles on real estate investing and has spoken at many events across the country teaching real estate valuation. He is the founder of InvestorCompsOnline.com, the best valuation training and real estate data source on the entire Internet. A recognized coach and mentor to thousands of investors nationwide, he founded an appraisal company in 1999 and soon after found his true gift was analyzing property value for real estate investors. Once Mark began investing himself, the floodgates opened. Within the last five years, he has been able to close real estate transactions totaling in the millions and maintains a substantial net worth. Most of which Mark used little or none of his own money and has never signed for a loan. You can learn to do it too! He is fondly known as "MJ in my PJ's" because he does all his investing from home.

Go to www.InvestorCompsOnline.com and click Get my Free Report and eBook KnowYourARV.com. The eBook is my gift to you full of valuable tips and tactics to know how to do deals quickly and make your profit when you buy!!!!

How to Effectively Deal with the Bad Stuff

MARLENE GREEN

So you feel like you are about to have a nervous breakdown or melt-down and want to go curl up in a corner because your best laid plans just went awry!

Or perhaps you feel like getting a gun to take yourself out, or the guys or gals who wiped out a good chunk of your hard-earned money and sucked up time that you will never get back.

Maybe you are suffering silently in quiet desperation because your future looks really dark, and you feel overwhelmed, absolutely paralyzed, and like an utter failure because the project you poured your time, money, heart, and energy into for months or years just went down the tubes! Nothing to show for your efforts…

Let's Talk about "The Bad Stuff": business deals gone bad, former business partners and friends now your worst enemies, a chunk of your net worth gone up in smoke, properties lost to foreclosure, employees and contractors gone lame, frighteningly low bank account balances, credit cards and credit lines maxed out, your best customers defect, nasty, and long drawn out litigation, and your spouse is fed up with you because you haven't had sex or been out on a date in over 13 months!

So how are you supposed to deal with all this Bad Stuff and be the peak performer we know you can be?

First, recognize that EVERY successful entrepreneur and business owner has had Really Bad Stuff happen at some point in his or her life. Yes, even the ones who look like their lives are perfect in every way, they exude success, money just comes to them, and they seem to have no worries. Trust me, they have had Bad Stuff, or have Bad Stuff going on now, and they hide it really well! Just know that you are not alone and that you will get through it.

Also realize that most people don't talk about the Bad Stuff from their past because it is so painful and it was such a dark and depressing time in their lives. I feel very strongly that we (as entrepreneurs and business owners) should talk about the Bad Stuff because the worst thing possible is feeling like a total failure as the only person on the planet who screwed up royally or never seems to accomplish anything.

We can also learn from other people's Bad Stuff to avoid taking that same journey through the dark period.

So, what does a peak performer do when Bad Stuff Happens?

1. Learn from and Model the Best Entrepreneurs on the Planet: I gain many insights and take comfort when I read the writings and biographies of successful folks who I truly admire like Richard Branson, Donald Trump, Dan Kennedy, Oprah Winfrey, Russell Simmons, Earl Graves, John Paul DeJoria, Nido Qubein, T. Boone Pickens, Ted Turner, and Cathy Hughes. Pay special attention to **how** they dealt with challenges and tough situations throughout their lives. Tune in to what conversations they were having with themselves as they dealt with the Bad Stuff. Though they seem to live a charmed life, the reality is that every one of them has had their ups and downs. No one is ever up 100% of the time.

2. Compartmentalize the Bad Stuff and Stay Focused on Solutions: When you are dealing with Bad Stuff, it tends to cast a dark cloud over EVERYTHING you are thinking and doing daily. It paralyzes you. So you have to make a conscious effort to put it in a box and schedule time to deal with and worry about it. Then go focus on finding solutions that will dig you out of the hole or get you out of that dark tunnel. You cannot afford to allow the Bad Stuff to consume 100% of your time and mental energy. That's toxic and a great way to get nowhere fast. Schedule Time to Think and Schedule Time to Worry. Most importantly, Get Stuff Done and Be Productive...Everyday.

3. Find a Confidante and Discuss Your Situation with Them: Just Be Careful who you Confide in (follow your gut) and make sure it's someone who can give you constructive, honest advice and encouragement. Look to mentors, members of your mastermind group or inner circle, and other successful entrepreneurs you have access to for counsel.

4. Take Time to Gain Clarity on what Your Measure is of Success, Happiness, Financial Security, Great Health, Peace of Mind, Enough Cash in the Bank, and Living a Life of Significance. With clarity on these things, you can regroup and move towards them on purpose. Maintain a Gratitude Journal that will help put your mind in a state of abundance, as opposed to that of lack and "woe is me."

5. Laugh about It! Develop a sense of humor about your troubles and how you got into the situation in the first place. Swear you will never fall for that crap again! Know that one day you will look back and laugh about it, so why not start laughing now? You are smarter and wiser and aware of the pitfalls to watch out for. Lesson learned…and you will never forget that living nightmare, ever. Also, the Bad Stuff stories are the best stories to share and laugh about with others as time passes. Chances are others will have a worse Bad Stuff story than you do!

6. Never Assume that Others Have a Better Life than You Because they Have Money! People with money still have all sorts of trials and tribulations going on in their lives with names like: Cancer, Autism, Divorce, Drugs, Depression, Jail Time, Mental Abuse, and Alcoholism.

7. How Bad Can It Get? Think of the absolute worse things that can happen to you and how you would deal with them. Then work your butt off to make sure you don't get there. If you do get there, you will know how to deal with it because you have a plan. Always have a Plan B.

8. Focus on What YOU Have Control Over. Reality is that you only have control over what you can do so get busy doing all that YOU CAN DO. Don't wait on or rely on other people to do things to solve your problems. They have their own agenda – for themselves. Chances are it was circumstances out of your control and the actions of others that contributed to your Bad Stuff. Focus on Actively Getting Things Done for Yourself and Get Busy Taking Care of #1. No one else will!

9. Expect to Work Hard and Put in the Time Necessary to Turn Things Around. Never underestimate the amount of work, time, energy, and effort it will take to get rid of or away from the Bad Stuff. The Good News is that you will get closer to your goals.

10. Do What You Know needs to be Done About Your Situation.
DECIDE to get things done now and stop worrying, being angry, and meditating on your Bad Stuff. The magnitude of your Bad Stuff will get bigger in your own mind and you will remain paralyzed. Break things down into small tasks and take steps to get things done daily. Free yourself by starting to take action and move fast on decisions to change things.

11. Regarding Money Loss…Get a grip on yourself and try to deal with things objectively. Don't delude yourself into thinking that things will clear up on their own. They won't. Yes, it's emotionally devastating to lose a pile of money and damage your business and personal credit or file bankruptcy, but this too shall pass, and is just a phase that you have to pass through. Consider how many now super-successful entrepreneurs have lost it all and filed bankruptcy, only to make a big comeback! Checkout Donald Trump's book, *Art of the Comeback*.

Deal with your creditors upfront. Get a Reality Check on your Cash Flow – How much is coming in and how much is going out? Cut back where necessary and seek to eliminate debt, no matter how long it takes. Don't Borrow anymore and keep piling up more Debt.

Have a Plan. Go Sell Something to Get to Cash Fast. Accept that we are all Salespeople so Suck it Up and Start Selling. Make it your mission to get customers for life and take great care of them so that they will take care of you, for life.

Also, Never Forget That "Cash is King" and that "Free and Clear" on all Assets is truly the Best Thing!

12. Become A Good Steward of Your Own Money and Your Business' Money. Recognize and accept that no one else will be a good steward of your money. Many times I have lulled myself into thinking that others will watch out for my pocket and have gotten burned big time, every time. Don't ever fall for this false sense of security.

13. Never Compare Yourself to Others Especially When You Are Down Dealing with Your Bad Stuff. Way too depressing and unproductive. As Nat King Cole says, "Pick yourself up, dust yourself off and start all over again." Simply go about Bettering Your Best and Striving for Excellence no matter how long it takes and if it means starting over from scratch, again.

Go about being outstanding in all that you do on your life's journey and if you come up short, learn from it, and never give up. Ignore the critics, detractors and naysayers. They have Bad Stuff too! Persistence and vowing to never give up on yourself (despite the Bad Stuff) is critical.

14. Most Importantly, *Always Be Marketing, Always Be Selling, and Promoting Something…Everyday.* Never lose sight of this! As long as you are consistently marketing and selling, you will have enough deal flow and incoming resources to deal with all the Bad Stuff that inevitably happens in life. I have personally dropped the ball on this one and have vowed never to make this mistake again…way too costly!

Finally, keep a cool head and rise above all the Bad Stuff because life is way too short to be down in the dumps for too long. Put things into perspective and remember that this too shall pass. As long as you keep moving forward and remain persistent, the Bad Stuff will become a thing of the past. *Hang in there, Stay Focused and Keep Your Chin Up!*

MARLENE GREEN is an entrepreneur, business strategist, and author of *How We Got Screwed*, as well as the chapter director of Glazer-Kennedy Insider's Circle's Manhattan and Northern New Jersey Chapters and President/CEO of Millionaire Blueprints Media, which publishes the award-winning *Millionaire Blueprints Magazine*. Marlene is a master networker who enjoys providing fresh eyes and connecting the dots for her members and clients. She is a passionate crusader for the Lonely Entrepreneur and encourages you to join a mastermind group where ideas and strategies in marketing, business, and life management are discussed freely for everyone's benefit. Marlene confesses to being a seminar junkie and values learning from the best teachers in real estate, business, and marketing. She understands the cost of ignorance as there was a time when she had zero access to millionaire mentors who would share their wisdom and blueprints that when implemented would help her leapfrog to prosperity. A graduate of New York University, she spent ten years as a consultant for the Top 50 law firms and Fortune 100 companies and has traveled extensively throughout the United States, Europe, Africa, Asia, the Caribbean, South America, and Australia. She grew up in Kingston, Jamaica.

For a FREE Audio CD where Marlene and her Friends share nuggets from her book *How We Got Screwed in Business: 101 Harsh Lessons Learned to Make Sure YOU Don't Get Screwed in Business Like We Did*, you are welcome to visit www.MarleneGreen.com and share your thoughts on Marlene's blog.

Breaking the Rules

YAR ZUK

Marketing can be considered a tooth and nail battle for the attention of targeted customers. If your innovations do not irritate your competitors you are not being creative enough. A willingness to break with conventional rules and bring new products and services with specific advantages to market as fast as possible can be controversial. However, this skill can reward those who constantly seek opportunities for improvement.

Most professionals, dentists included, that get their start with a university degree find aggressive marketers and innovators are generally frowned upon. The professionals usually sit back and wait for manufacturers to develop the programs that that come along with a particular product that they buy. The reliance on stock marketing packages provided by manufacturers to promote their services is widespread in the dental profession.

As an example, Invisalign® is a billion dollar company which dentists can work with. Invisalign® is an advanced system which uses clear aligners to orthodontically straighten crooked teeth without braces. While this is an exciting concept, it also is a simple program for almost any dentist to offer after a weekend seminar. With the simplicity and low entrance barrier to become a provider of this service, a dentist's service is vulnerable to becoming a commodity and will be vulnerable to a price war.

A savvy marketing dentist may choose to put a twist on a company sponsored marketing package and make his/her program better, faster, or more convenient than the services of another professional. One way to do this is to invest in an independent marketing system like Dentistry for Diabetics® that helps an entrepreneur stand out from the crowd and offers an exclusive area. In this case, the program helps develop systems, which apply to treating a patient base with a specific set of dental problems (diabetics are at higher risk for gum disease and benefit from specialized care).

The customized systems include innovative promotions, which promote the advantages of the professional's individual program. A professional must be willing to step out of the usual friendly kinship among the peers and think like a competitor. Once you step out and start becoming more innovative this attitude usually kicks in naturally. By disassociating from the local association meetings you will be better able to think as an entrepreneur.

This competitive mindset will in turn also ready you for greater innovation. Prepare yourself to handle criticism and be able to dish it out if you want to be exceptionally successful. In a competitive market you must have your bulletproof armor on and hunt down your competitors ruthlessly like at a game of paintball.

In my case I took the position that, in general, orthodontic treatment takes too long and patients are in braces longer than they need to be. I also turned my sights on the cosmetic dentists knowing that they sometimes overuse veneers when other alternatives are more conservative and affordable. In short, I was picking a fight with some very powerful and well-organized groups.

By knowing your competition's weaknesses you can cut them down very effectively. This may take a large investment in time and money, in fact you may need to learn to do things the way they do it before you are able to truly offer a better alternative. In my case I learned to do veneers and orthodontics and found the weaknesses and strengths in each of the ways these treatments are used in cosmetic dentistry.

To be cutting edge you need to learn from the best of the best, and be ready to do things totally opposite of the way you were taught in college. While most professionals will rarely invest more than half a tank of gas to be exposed to new ideas, if you are willing to go the extra mile to rub elbows with the top guns in your field you will take your game to a higher level. This can result in innovations that you never dreamed of.

A professional can take the new ideas and then use them to develop his/her own brand. While some experts feel that this can take millions of dollars and the advice of high-priced marketing firms, this is not always true. You CAN establish your own brand identity in a small market by studying successful marketing styles in other industries.

One example of a controversial marketing idea for a professional is to use a cartoon character. We developed a little "Toothache" character that stood out like a sore thumb. Not that many professionals would stoop to this level, but the concept has been very successful. The little "Toothache Guy" has a swollen face and a telephone in hand. The simple caption "Toothache?" meets marketing expert Dan Kennedy's basic premise that a good ad should be able to stand alone with the headline and a phone number.

The use of a cartoon character also lends itself well to the promotional use of toys and mascots. Our Toothache mascot gets smiles at parades and mall walks, giving away toothbrushes and gifts (with our office name) as he skips along. The latest version we are looking into is a plush toy give-away that could be tied into a charity drive to raise money for a worthy cause or simply as a gift for younger grade school or kindergarten kids. A toy company like CustomPlushToys.com may be able to help you if you have a similar idea.

The Toothache cartoon is not just a pretty face; it takes things a step farther by agitating the viewer. The large infected swelling is clear evidence that neglecting a person's dental health a little too long can have painful consequences. Using a high-tech graphic would hardly have the same effect and would be less memorable.

Professionals who want to market their business need to know something about advertising agencies. As some of us have learned the hard way, an ad agency is not specifically interested in generating a response for the client. They are interested in making a "pretty" ad that looks pleasing and really do not care about effectiveness or brand building. An entrepreneur must always keep in mind that there is a level of separation from the aesthetic design of an ad and the features, which will generate more business for the person paying for the ad. Do your ads generate intense interest from a specific market segment?

High Speed Braces™ is an orthodontic program that I've helped develop that promises to reduce the time people need to wear braces. The name is simple and it reflects the advantage the system has over more traditional and slower styles of orthodontics. A second advantage that HSB offers to patients is a huge savings in price when compared to a full porcelain veneer makeover. While prices for a full mouth of veneers can often exceed $50,000 the High Speed Braces™ alternative can often be had for a tenth the price.

Another benefit that can be provided by "rapid orthodontics" is actually extremely powerful. What many people do not realize is that when dentists use veneers to straighten teeth they often have to grind away a significant amount of enamel in the process. This ugly secret within the profession can be exploited because we are not afraid of offending the competitors. High Speed Braces™ or any type of orthodontic treatment can be much more conservative and kinder to your teeth. Why shouldn't the public know about it?

A person outside the dental profession would have no idea what a hornet's nest a simple idea like **3 Month Braces**™ can stir up. First we came up with the idea and then we found a way to make it happen using some unusual formulas. These ideas were thought to be radical, dangerous, and almost insane. When an independent new article was recently released that stated, "faster braces are safer" it was music to our ears. Our systems were way ahead of the curve and have the potential to be dynamite.

By capitalizing on the support from the scientific data our brand becomes even more powerful and gains market share as the competitors fumble for answers. If the studies went the other way we'd be regrouping for another cage fight. Think of yourself as the Bruce Lee of your profession or industry. As you likely already know, Bruce came up with his own style of fighting. He disagreed with the classical styles which he had studied and blended ideas from many forms of martial arts. Bruce

Lee literally had to fight to prove his ideas had merit. In his time he was ridiculed by many but is remembered now as a legend.

The marketing watchmen of the professional governing bodies are often used to stifle the entrepreneurial few. While the goal of keeping advertising truthful is important, the problem is the associations sometimes cross the line and try to limit the freedom of expression of the individual members. By trying to make an even playing field the authorities attempt to stomp out any individuals that step out of line. A simple fact is not all professionals are created equal.

These lines or regulations are not set in stone, and each time they are revised to accommodate the concerns of one group within the profession another is violated by its restrictions. The greater the number of complaints you get from your peers the more likely you are doing something right.

If you become a student of marketing and learn the techniques that are effective from outside your area of expertise, with a little creativity you will be able to break rules and enter new frontiers. My involvement in the Glazer-Kennedy Peak Performer Mastermind has provided many new insights that have accelerated our program development.

DR. MICHAEL "YAR" ZUK is an inventor and a dental marketing expert who predicts conservative cosmetic dentists will be switching from porcelain veneers as their primary treatment to accelerated orthodontics. He develops marketing programs for dentists and has been featured on TRUMP U, selected as Dentist of the Month by GEMS Insider who called him a "marketing superstar," and Best Dentist in the City by a reader poll. He would like to thank his dental staff for their support, especially Yvonne for the nudge into ortho, his competitors for their constant prodding, his family for putting up with his numerous projects, his patients who settle for reasonable improvements, Cindy M. for being his first celebrity patient, his mom for encouraging creativity and his late father for his courage to do things that will attract controversy.

Resources:
www.HighSpeedBraces.org
www.3MonthBraces.com
www.KillerToothache.com

RECOMMENDED READING: *1000 GEMS* newsletter (dentists)

How to Build a Marketing Plan for Your Business

DIANE CONKLIN & GAIL SASEEN

Marketing, marketing, marketing. We hear it everywhere we go. And, why is that? Well, it's because marketing is the core of your business, no matter what business you're in.

Marketing can be defined as everything you do related to bringing clients and customers to you and your business, so you then have an opportunity to sell them your products and services. Marketing is the engine that makes your business run. Marketing is where you, the business owner, should be spending the majority of your time.

Marketing and sales are what generates the revenue in your business, and because of that, they are two of the most important things you do in your business on a day-to-day basis. Since marketing is so important to you and your business, it's critical for you to know how to build a marketing plan for your business.

One Marketing Plan or Multiple Plans

You definitely need an overall marketing plan for your business, and you also need to develop a marketing plan for every campaign, product, service, seminar, and activity in your business.

The devil is in the details, as they say, and if you will take the time to plan and detail the steps in each of your marketing campaigns, you will be on your way to a much smoother process, and your campaigns will be much more successful than if you take the approach of throwing mud on the wall to see what sticks.

The throw mud on the wall approach might be successful for a short while, and you might luck out and even have some profitable campaigns, but you will more than likely also have a lot of waste in your campaigns, and in the end, would have been much more successful – meaning you could have made a lot more money – had you taken the time to develop a plan from the beginning.

So, the bottom line is, your company will need multiple marketing plans. You will want one overall plan, that will just give you the bullets of what you're planning on doing for the whole year, or maybe the quarter, and then more detailed plans for each and every item on your master plan.

Your overall marketing plan will be sort of a big picture type plan. It will highlight the things you are planning on doing throughout the year. For example, the yearly picture might include plans for holding two of your own seminars during the year, eight teleseminars, one new product launch, ten speaking engagements at other marketers/promoters events, one high level coaching program, a mastermind program, and so on.

Then, each of those individual items would have their own detailed marketing plan. The individual plan would include the specific details of exactly when and what you will be doing to market that program.

The Keys to Developing a Good Marketing Plan

The real key to all of this is what is called backward planning. In other words, start with the end in mind and develop your marketing plan in the reverse order than what the plan will be executed in.

Another key to putting together your marketing plan is to know what media you intend to utilize in your campaigns. It's important not to rely too heavily on any one media, but to include multiple media types in your marketing plans.

Keys To A Good Marketing Plan:

1) Backward Planning
2) Multiple Media
3) Message to Market Match

Your marketing plan might include email campaigns, direct mail, teleseminars or webinars, joint venture arrangements, voice blasts, text messaging, fax blasts, and telemarketing (check with your attorney to see about the laws in your area and make sure you are in compliance, if you plan to include faxing or calling people in your marketing plans). Depending on your business model, you might also include radio, television, or newspaper advertising in your marketing campaigns.

One is always the worst number, so you never want to employ only one media type in your campaigns. Instead, you want a multi-pronged approach in all of your marketing.

One easy way to think about marketing is like a stool you sit on. It would be tough to balance a stool if it only had one or two legs, but three legs are more stable and if it had four legs, it would be even more stable and secure. If you have a four-legged stool, and one leg broke or fell off, you could still sit on that stool pretty comfortably. On the other hand, if you started out sitting on a three-legged stool, and one gets broken off, you'd have some difficulty staying upright on the stool.

Marketing is much the same way. If your marketing plan includes only email and direct mail, for a particular campaign, and your mail doesn't get delivered for some reason (like there is a natural disaster or something else happens) or let's say it does get delivered, but it doesn't work for some reason and you don't make very many sales, now, you're down to only one media for your marketing.

If, however, you are using email, direct mail, fax, classified ads, online article submissions, and joint ventures, and one or two of those don't work, you still have options. The chances of none of your marketing medias working, or all of them being ineffective at the same time, are much smaller when you're using multiple media outlets rather than only one.

Message to Market Match

One other thing you always want to make sure of, in your marketing, is that you have a message to market match. The more specific your message is to your particular market, the better your results will be. And, a very specific, targeted niche market to send your messages to will also increase your marketing results.

Think of it as a triangle, with each point of the triangle being one of these three things, either market, message, or media, and you will more easily understand the connection between these three very important marketing factors. This will look something like:

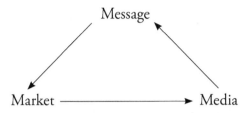

Putting Your Marketing Plan Together

Now you have all the steps, you know all the variables and things to consider as you're putting your plan together, so now it's time to actually put your plan to paper, or calendar – whichever you find works best for you.

Remember, this all starts with backward planning, so go to the date of your event, launch, teleseminar, or whatever it is you are devising your marketing plan for, and work back from there.

You might want to begin by planning for your direct mail pieces and build the rest of your marketing funnel around that. For example, let's call your event date X, and let's say you want the last piece of mail to be in your client, or prospects, hands two weeks before the event, then you have to plan on mailing the piece three to five days prior to the two week point, because it will typically take that long after you put the piece in the mail to reach your clients. So, the first item on your calendar will be on the date that represents X minus 19 days. (So, if your event is scheduled for December 20th, X minus 19 is December 1st.) That is the day your last mail piece must go in the mail.

Now, you just continue on, working backwards and adding all your direct mail plans to the calendar. Once you have that media finished, and you're satisfied with that part of the campaign, then simply go back to the calendar and add the additional media you're going to use into your campaign.

Whether you're doing this on an electronic calendar or a paper calendar, you might find it helpful to use color-coding to help make it easier to read once you've completed this exercise. So, for example, all the direct mail actions might be in yellow, your email campaigns might be in blue, your voice blasts might be listed in red, and your faxes might be in green.

Big Ideas:

1) Have a Marketing Plan
2) Use Systems
3) Implement and Execute

Using a system like this, or something similar, that makes sense to you, will make it much easier to look at your plan and be able to quickly distinguish the different parts of the campaign. It will also help you know what's coming up that you need to be preparing for.

Now, when you look at your calendar or plan, you can easily see what needs to be done in the coming days or weeks, to complete your marketing plan. You might need to make sure the printer has the mail piece completed, and it's been delivered to the mail house, or that all the emails have been loaded in your database management system, and are ready to go out, or you might need to write some copy.

Whatever it is, the marketing task at hand will be much easier with your plan in front of you and your staff, so everyone knows where you are in your plan and what their part is in the process.

Following this system, for developing your marketing plans, will make your campaigns run smoother and will make the running of your campaigns much easier – for you, or whoever is in charge of the execution of the campaigns.

After all, we're all in the marketing business, so no matter what you're business in, you'll need to be developing campaigns like this to keep your business growing and flourishing. Some will be simple and some will be more complex, but if you start with the basics in mind, you'll be a lot more successful with every campaign.

DIANE CONKLIN and GAIL SASEEN are business owners, entrepreneurs, marketing coaches, and consultants who assist small business owners in the development of smart marketing plans and strategies for their businesses that allow those businesses to go to the next level. They've been in the information marketing business for over ten years, and have earned their reputations as executors – that means they know how to get things done! Diane is a direct response marketing expert who specializes in showing small business owners, entrepreneurs, coaches, and consultants how to integrate their marketing strategies, media, and methods, to get maximum results from their marketing dollars. She is also an event planning expert. She has planned and produced events grossing over $1,000,000. Gail specializes in coaching and consulting with entrepreneurs in the information marketing business with solutions to business challenges, affordable marketing strategies, product development, affiliate program management, list generation and management practices. Through their company, Complete Marketing Systems, Diane and Gail offer a wide range of programs and services – from direct response marketing, strategic planning, list building and management strategies, copywriting, direct mail, fast product development, staff training, systems development, implementation techniques to seminar, workshop and event marketing, planning, and management.

To claim a free sample marketing plan and other free gifts go to www.peakperformersbook.com or give them a call at (866) 293-0589.

Gangster Marketing

ED CLAY

Every business, no matter what it is, comes down to sales and marketing. It's rather simple yet can be so difficult to grasp.

My good friend and mentor, Lloyd Irvin, once told me, "Good marketing can sell a non existing product, bad marketing can't sell free gold."

I've had a lot of ups and downs in business. Some things I've hit right on the head and some things I've missed by a mile. The one thing that stays true is what I call Gangster Marketing. Gangster Marketing is more than just marketing, it's a way of life. It's eating, sleeping, and breathing the marketing in your business every day and hour of your life. It's a ruthless and somewhat reckless means of marketing your business, where as the public looks at your company, there's no doubt that your business stands out from the competition.

To be a Gangster Marketer you have to have brass balls. The competition will probably hate you because you think outside the box. The truth is it doesn't matter what they think and the more they hate you the better job you're doing.

A Gangster Marketer is fearless in his marketing campaigns. I've done many things that I've been proud of in marketing, but one clear example of fearlessly crossing the line and being a total Gangster Marketer is when a local newspaper, the *Nashville Scene*, was doing their "Best of

Nashville" showcasing the "best" business's in my area. In reality it was nothing more than a voting contest that I didn't want any part of. They wanted me to get a bunch of my students to go out and get signatures saying we were the best Martial Arts School. It seemed like a lot of work so I simply took out a full-page ad in the paper proclaiming myself as the best in Nashville and went on the attack of the winner, exposing the paper for its joke of a voting policy and him for his embarrassing ad bragging about being the "best" in Nashville. Of all the ads I've written, it is still one of my favorites!

Before you become a Gangster Marketer, you need to know that you are going to make enemies. Very few people are okay with this. Here are some things you can do to start your first Gangster Marketing campaign.

1. Develop your USP in a controversial way. Your USP means everything in your business. It's the lifeline that makes your company run. Many company's don't even have a USP and don't know what a USP is. An example for my MMA gym is that we're the only real self-defense program in Middle Tennessee. My current ad headline is "Warning!!! Karate Will Get You Killed."

    By developing a controversial Gangster USP you allow yourself to get even more attention than just a regular USP. News of controversy spreads fast. Your company can immediately stick out like a sore thumb, which is something you want with any business. Many people are afraid to ruffle feathers, but a true Gangster USP is the easiest way to get attention on your company fast!

2. Go directly after the competition. I go on blast ad smear campaigns telling how bad the competition is and how we kick their ass in every aspect of business. It's natural for people to not want confrontation, but as a Gangster Marketer you are not afraid of confrontation. Rather, you are known as someone who is happy to throw down if someone wants to fight.

3. If they are a business owned by a man, attack his manhood. No man likes to be questioned as a man. Hopefully, the company will fire back an ad against you. This will give you free advertising and allow you to follow up with another ad. This is a true Gangster approach but you have the advantage because you know exactly what angle you're coming from.

4. Don't be afraid when doing your guerilla marketing campaigns to put up marketing right next to the competition. When I do street signs for real estate or my gym, I'll often have my staff put signs right in front of the competitions business. If the competition doesn't take the sign down in a timely manner, their customers will now see you. From this you know that you already have a prospect that is interested in your product or service. You are basically advertising right in front of their business, which gets you access to their customers.

5. Advertise in the same mediums as the competition. Have your ad downplay the competitions strengths. If you know the competition is saying they are great in one area, it's easy to show actual weaknesses in that area. With some thought it's also easy to say why your company is even better in that area than they are. This strategy has worked very well for me over the years and is something that I think anyone with creativity can use.

6. Have a section on your website with your company versus the competition. List all your qualities and then list their inaccuracies. If you go to www.nashvillemma.com you will see a button that says us versus others. In this section I go over every possible strength that we have over the competition. It's somewhat crushing to any competitor because we highlight our strengths and their weaknesses in great detail. An example from the website is:

Nashville MMA vs. the Other MMA Schools

"You will find amazing wrestlers and judo practitioners at Ed Clay's Nashville MMA. NMMA is known around the country for possessing very strong takedowns and its instructors have utilized them against the world's best submission wrestlers! NMMA head instructors learned to wrestle from certified wrestling coaches, Division I College Wrestlers, Judo Black Belts, and world-class wrestlers! We have students that were members of international teams as well as NCAA all Americans!

Unfortunately, a lot of grapplers learn their takedowns from Brazilian Jiu-Jitsu and any educated grappler can tell you that BJJ has weak takedowns – their specialty is once the fights hits the ground, not before! Just watch their classes. Their advanced students begin all their submission matches from their knees! This is a practice only done by beginners at NMMA – all our students with over three months training begin from their feet. And if an MMA school does have strong takedowns – sometimes they end up not having good jiu-jitsu or bad striking."

I have numerous examples on this website so feel free to check it out.

7. Have a Gangster lead generating website. The Internet is by far the best place for me to get my message out. Every bit of Gangster Marketing I do funnels them to call me or to my website. Once I get a potential customer to my website, my goal is to get them to give me their information. It's imperative in the 21st century that your company has a website that catches peoples attention. You want your website to be so annoying with your message that they feel bad if they don't give you their information. If you do not have a good online presence, you will not be a successful company.

8. Hire a good SEO company to dominate the top ad searches online. Good Search Engine Optimization is key to running a successful website. When someone types in a key word search on Google or other search engines, you want to be at the top of the field. A good SEO company can help you get your desired results quickly and effectively.

9. Hire a good AdWord company to maximize your AdWord campaigns. There are many good AdWord companies that are part of Glazer/Kennedy groups. I really can't say which one is the best, but I can assure you they will save you money if you're currently advertising on Google or Yahoo. They have ways of figuring out which key words are the best in your group and which key words you shouldn't be using. Many times companies spend too much money per click and are getting clicks from people who aren't in their target market. As in any specialty field, it's important to hire an expert company.

10. Diligently track your advertising and with lightning speed drop all advertising that isn't working and put more into what is. As Glazer/Kennedy teaches us, money is attracted to speed. This includes dropping your ads as soon as you know they're not working. To be able to drop ads quickly you must track your advertising very closely. I for one have slipped on this only to find out months later I was wasting money on ads that were not working or headlines that were ineffective.

11. Make sure you get other "Gangsters" in your business to be raving testimonials for your products and service. I love testimonials, but what I love even more is to get testimonials from celebrities in your business that people will recognize. These are what I call "Gangster" testimonials. If you are close to anyone that people know, the thing that can set your company apart is a celebrity that will vouch for how great you are. It's hard to put a price tag on what this is worth.

12. Make sure speed is your focus on all of your marketing efforts. You can clean up any mistakes in the future but the idea is to get information about your product or service to the public as quickly as possible. Speed is the most important thing in any marketing campaign. I constantly see people wasting time trying to get things perfect when they could easily put out what they currently have and worry about perfecting it at a later date. In most cases, what you currently have is better than nothing at all. And a lot of time what you thought was a perfect ad had no effectiveness.

These 12 simple tips on how to run a "Gangster Marketing" campaign are sure to help any business explode. I'm a simple person and I hope that my message will help you grow your business into whatever you want it to be. The only question you have to ask yourself is: are you Gangster enough?

Ed Clay started his martial arts training at the age of 11. He was undefeated as a professional MMA fighter and was ranked as high as 9 in the world by the Shooto organization. At the age of 20 he opened two businesses: Nashville Mixed Martial Arts and Gameness Fightwear. Nashville MMA is now one of the largest MMA schools in the country and Gameness Fightwear is the largest supplier of Brazilian Jiu-Jitsu uniforms in the world. Both of these companys have been a business TN top 50 company as one of the 50 fastest growing company's in the state.

As an MMA trainer Ed has trained fighters fighting in the largest events in the world including the Ultimate Fighting Championships, Pride, M1, and Dream. He has been interviewed in many martial arts publications and written articles for Submission Fighter, Grappling and Tapout Magazines.

Ed has also had huge success in Real Estate investing in the United States and international markets. With his Real Estate knowledge he has traveled the country doing real estate seminars teaching everything from short sales to buying property with no money down. For the last seminar tour he went on he taught how to buy property in international markets focusing on Costa Rica.

Ed currently lives in Nashville, TN where he spends most of his time training his fighters.

For more free Gangster Marketing tips go to www.gangstermarketing.com and sign up for my free newsletter. If you liked this chapter check out my book called "Gangster Business" at www.gangsterbusiness.com.

The Power and Versatility of 24/7 Recorded Message Hotlines

PAUL CHAMPANERIA

For over 20 years now, 24/7-recorded message hotlines have been one of the best-kept secrets of successful marketers and entrepreneurs. Savvy marketing teachers like Dan Kennedy saw and understood the explosive leverage of 24/7 recorded messages early on, but even with Dan's enthusiasm and stamp of approval there are only a small fraction of entrepreneurs using them effectively. By putting 24/7 recorded message hotlines to work for your business, you'll experience firsthand the power and versatility of this low-cost and easy-to-use marketing tool, and see just how easily it can increase your sales, while saving you time and money.

I first began using 24/7 recorded message hotlines in 1991, at the age of 16, while working as a distributor for a multilevel marketing company. By putting the leveraging power of these easy-to-use hotlines to work for me and my team, I was able to rapidly become one of the company's top distributors. I have since gone on to build an entire business around 24/7 recorded message hotlines, with my main goal being to help more entrepreneurs learn about and implement this great marketing tool in their businesses.

What are 24/7 recorded message hotlines?

24/7 recorded message hotlines are a type of voice-mail system that allows you to record messages that your prospects can listen to 24 hours a day, 7 days a week, 365 days a year. They simply call your hotline number and receive your message(s).

Using a 24/7-recorded message hotline lets you educate your prospects in an automated, robotic way about why they should do business with you. After your prospect has listened to your message, they normally have the option to either leave a message for you, with their contact info, or be connected/forwarded to a live person.

How do 24/7 recorded message hotlines work?

The quickest way to put 24/7 recorded message hotlines to work for your business is to use a simple two- or three-line ad that offers important and useful information and then closes with your recorded message hotline number.

Example:

Bob runs an ad for his home contractor business in which he states:

"Warning! Don't call any home contractor until you listen to this free recorded message. Call XXX-XXX-XXXX extension XXX anytime."

When prospects call Bob's hotline, they then hear helpful information about things like "5 Mistakes to Avoid When Choosing a Home Contractor" or "7 Questions to Ask Before Inviting a Home Contractor to Your Home." After listening to the message, they can leave their contact information to learn more, or be connected/forwarded directly to Bob or one of Bob's staff.

These types of ads can work no matter what type of business you're in, and can be easily adjusted to work in just about any advertising medium – classifieds, Yellow Pages, postcards, direct mail promotions, Web promotions, or even billboard ads. You need only change the terminology of the ad to fit your particular business.

What can 24/7-recorded message hotlines do for my business?

A 24/7-recorded message hotline enables you to reach out to your prospects, customers, and clients around the clock in a non-threatening and credible way. Many people are hesitant to call and speak to a live person for fear of getting a pushy salesperson on the other end with a high-pressure sales pitch. But with a recorded message you allay their fears, since a recorded message is not threatening. At the same time, you increase your business's credibility, since a recorded message is accessible to everyone.

Studies show that a publicly accessible recorded message is perceived by callers to be much more believable and credible than a live salesperson delivering a pitch.

In addition, using 24/7-recorded message hotlines saves you huge amounts of time, since the system sifts, sorts, and screens out prospects who do not have a high level of interest. Because of this built-in screening process you are assured of getting pre-qualified, warm prospects rather than time wasting "tire kickers" who are merely window shopping.

As Dan mentions in his book *No B.S. Business Success*:

> "Offering additional information to prospective customers via a free recorded message compared with requiring prospects to call a regular business number and talk with a live salesperson almost always boosts response. At the same time, the recorded message lets you, the marketer, run ads, send out mailings, and handle all the initial response without any significant staff requirements and without having to take calls personally."

24/7-recorded message hotlines are a low-cost and effective way to put a key component of your marketing on autopilot and avoid cold calling, while freeing up your valuable time for other areas of your business.

10 Tips for using 24/7-recorded message hotlines effectively

Tip #1: Long messages can work well.
Many people believe that recorded messages must be short, but this is a myth. Long messages work amazingly well, provided they are not boring. As long as you have interesting information to share, people will listen to it, even if it takes several minutes.

It's extremely important to test and adjust. A good 24/7-recorded message hotline system lets you review your call reports to find out what percentage of your callers are leaving a message or connecting directly to you. By using these reports, you'll be able to quickly tell if people are hanging up mid-message and whether or not you should change or edit it.

Tip #2: No need to ask for your caller's phone number.

With a good 24/7-recorded message service, there is no need to ask for your prospect's phone number. Why? Because a good service will have an unblockable caller ID feature that will automatically gather the caller's phone number when they call. You only need to ask for their name and address and/or email address. Studies have shown that response goes up when people are not required to leave their phone number.

Tip #3: Give hot prospects the option to connect directly to you after listening to your message.

You normally have a choice about whether or not people can connect directly to you after listening to your message, and you should always give people the option to do so. With enhanced call forwarding and find me features, 24/7-recorded message hotline services make it easy for you to take the call, no matter where you are.

Tip #4: Make your business card a direct response magnet.

Put an ad for your 24/7-recorded message hotline on the back of your business card and see how much more powerful your business card becomes.

Tip #5: Get feedback and gather testimonials.

Put your recorded hotline number on all your products and use it as a 24/7-feedback line. You can also use this feedback line to solicit testimonials from satisfied customers.

Tip #6: Increase response from your Yellow Pages advertising.

Drastically increase the response to your Yellow Pages ad by using a 24/7-recorded message hotline in your ad. You'll also reduce your Yellow Pages advertising budget, since you can use a smaller ad and get the same or better response than you would with a larger ad. Moreover, a good 24/7-recorded message services allows you to easily track response from your advertising, so you can see just how well your ad is performing.

Tip #7: Include your hotline number, even if you have a lead generation website in your advertising.

According to recent statistics, 27% of Americans still do not have Internet access (outside the U.S. the number is significantly higher). So it makes good sense to include both your 24/7-recorded message hotline number and your website address.

Tip #8: Survey your customers.

A good 24/7-recorded message hotline service provides a Q&A feature that allows you to perform surveys and find out exactly what your customers think about your company, products, services, etc. This is a great tool for quality assurance. You can also do new product surveys to find out what kinds of products your customers want from you.

Tip #9: Track return on investment (ROI) for your advertising.

Save tons of money on advertising by tracking ROI through the handy ad tracking feature provided by your 24/7-recorded message hotline service. This tool allows you to see exactly what the response is for certain ads and to adjust accordingly.

Here's how it works in a nutshell:

Bob wants to track which specific ads are bringing in the calls to his 24/7-recorded message hotline. So he simply assigns an extension for each ad and/or promotion he is running and includes that extension in his advertising.

For example, he gives his newspaper classified ad extension 1300, his trade journal classified ad extension 1301, and his direct mail promotion extension 1302.

When callers first call in to Bob's hotline they are directed to dial the specific extension from the ad they saw. In the event that Bob wants to make things slightly easier for his callers, he could instead have separate phone numbers for each of his ads, rather than one number with separate extensions. By assigning each of his ads an extension number, Bob will now be able to look at his call reports and see exactly how much response each of his ads is generating.

Tip #10: Include the words "Free Recorded Message" in your ad.
Our studies have shown that response is much higher when these three words are included in your ad. Just mentioning that it's a toll-free number is not enough.

Important message for leaders in MLM organizations:

As I mentioned previously, I rapidly became one of the top distributors in an MLM company, thanks to the leveraging power of 24/7-recorded message hotlines. As a leader in an MLM organization, you know how important it is to generate high-quality leads for telephone follow-up in order to build a strong distribution team.

Many MLM organizations are finding that leads generated through 24/7-recorded message hotlines are of better quality than leads generated through websites. For example, phone numbers gathered through websites are not always accurate, whereas with 24/7-recorded message hotlines, you will always get the prospect's correct phone number. Place your hotline number in classified ads, on postcards, on flyers, and even on your website.

In addition, you can equip your entire team with 24/7-recorded message hotlines and prerecorded messages and scripts to provide a turnkey lead generation system. You can also use the system to communicate with your team via regular voice broadcasts. This is a great way to mentor and train newly recruited members of your team.

To listen to a special informational training MP3 and learn more about using 24/7-recorded message hotlines for your MLM business visit http://www.TeleCenterDirectSales.com.

Important message for leaders of Information Marketing Coaching Groups and Companies:

If you are in the business of coaching others (professionals, business owners, real estate agents, etc) on how to get more customers and clients, you can make your members' lives even easier by offering them turnkey recorded message hotline packages.

Each of these hotline packages could include such things as training modules that focus specifically on their niche along with appropriate prerecorded messages, prewritten scripts, and "cookie cutter" marketing materials.

Important message for Real Estate Agents:

24/7-recorded message hotlines offer a surefire method for getting more listings and selling more homes. They help you lock in more listings with your listing presentation, and provide a 24/7 listing tool with an instant contact option. They are also a great tool for building a list of prospective sellers. And best of all, they allow you to weed out unfavorable prospects so you deal only with genuinely interested buyers. To learn more about using 24/7 real estate hotlines to get more listings and sell more properties visit http://www.TeleCenterRealEstate.com.

PAUL CHAMPANERIA is the founder and CEO of COA Network, Inc., a provider of 24-hour recorded message hotlines, virtual phone services, and online marketing systems located in Piscataway, New Jersey. As one of the first independent voicemail service providers to create his own communications software, Paul achieved landmark independence in the telephony industry. He has worked diligently to develop new and exciting telecommunication and marketing tools for entrepreneurs, direct sales team leaders, real estate agents, coaching companies, and mobile sales forces. With over 17 years' combined leadership in marketing, programming, and product development, Paul's entrepreneurial success and acknowledged expertise place him in the top echelon in his industry.

Paul Champaneria is the CEO of COA Network www.COANetwork.com, the leading provider of Toll-Free 24/7 Recorded Message Hotlines. To receive more tips on how this great marketing tool can help accelerate your business, and to take a 14-day full-featured, no-cost, no-risk test drive, go to www.RecordedMessageHotlines.com.

How to Shortcut Your Way to Success by Being a "Right Hand Man"

DAVID DUBEAU

My name is Dave Dubeau, and in just two years, I have become the proud co-owner of a membership business with over 2,000 members across Canada and over one million dollars per year in revenues. I also earn a six-figure retainer to be the marketing director for a nationally known speaker in Canada, who operates with a marketing budget of over two million dollars per year. I've accomplished this without having to create a customer list or spend hundreds of thousands, perhaps millions, of dollars creating a quality database to work from.

I say this not to brag (well, maybe just a little), but to demonstrate that you can be involved in an information marketing business without having to be the "star." Just like I did.

I've been a Dan Kennedy junkie since 1995 when I first discovered him as a Canadian ex-patriot running my own language training school in Costa Rica in Central America. I knew Kennedy's ideas worked: in a market of over 50 competitors, his concepts helped me take my struggling business from the bottom of the heap into the top three within two years. His teachings helped me create a successful business and a great lifestyle that I enjoyed for several years.

I found myself in a quandary when I moved my Costa Rican wife and family back to Canada in 2003. After 10 years overseas, I returned home with no contacts, no credit history, and no business prospects. I floundered around for a couple of years, rapidly depleting my savings and getting into some serious credit card debt. I tried my hand at "creative" real estate, advertising sales, and consulting but never managed to make any serious money. After being immersed in Dan Kennedy's teachings for so long, I longed to get involved in information marketing.

My original idea was to create a "business in a box" that would assist others in starting a language school overseas—ideal for ex-pats, English teachers, and travelers (or so I thought). I immediately went to work and put together a course with audio CDs. I worked for months on it, but I was increasingly concerned about the cost of marketing and advertising (I was broke, remember?).

In early 2006, after spending hours racking my brain, trying to think of a person (with a ready database of customers) with whom I could team up. An acquaintance of mine came to mind, Darren Weeks. Darren, a national speaker in Canada, promotes his Canadian version of Robert Kiyosaki's *Rich Dad, Poor Dad* philosophy of financial education.

I had been to Darren's events and I was in his database. He would come to a city, put on an event, and leave everyone excited, ready to take on the world. Darren is a very good speaker, and he actually does what he recommends to people; he is an active businessman and investor. Unlike a lot of public speakers, he actually "walks his talk." However, I had noticed that he didn't communicate with his database of event attendees as effectively as he could. After his events, he would not return to that city for six to 12 months; in the meanwhile, there was very little communication, and people would lose that spark that he had left them with in the first place.

Originally, I thought about approaching him with the idea of a joint venture to promote my language-school-in-a-box to his database. When I realized that response would be minimal at best, the light bulb finally went off in my head. Forget about the language thing, I thought. Create an information product specifically for Darren's database. Like Kennedy so often says, find the "herd" and then create something for them. I decided to S&D (swipe and deploy) Kennedy's proven model of an "inner circle" and create the "Fast Track Inner Circle" membership program.

It seemed like a good idea to me, but I had to convince Darren to work with me on it. I outlined the whole program for him: "Canadianized" Rich Dad, Poor Dad information and education via a monthly newsletter (with multiple writers, so he wouldn't have to write very much), a monthly audio CD (that I would provide), teleseminars (we would do jointly), and a members-only website (that I would manage). I made it very hard for him to say no; I would take care of all the details, including production and delivery, and he would simply write a monthly article and promote the program at his live events.

I had done business with Darren previously, so he already knew me. I pitched him the idea with an e-mail that said something like, "Darren, how would you like to make an extra $10,000 a month with next to no effort?" He answered fairly quickly, and we talked about the idea over the phone.

He said that if I was interested in pursuing it, I should fly across the country and launch the idea at one of his live events. I remembered some of Kennedy's advice: see if there is a market for a product, sell it, and then create it. So that is what I did. I flew from British Columbia to Toronto and pitched the idea to a group of about 300 people. Sixty-seven of them signed up for the program immediately. With 67 registration forms in hand, I returned home and went to work creating the program.

First, I found some contributing writers. I used some of the contacts that Darren had, and I also went out and found some experts myself. Still, eight writers and 12 pages later, our first newsletter was a pretty "skinny" affair. Today, we have people literally lining up to be "experts." I currently have 17 regular writers contributing articles on business, real estate, and investing from a Canadian perspective (as things work a little differently up here North of the border).

Soon I noticed that Darren's general marketing was not as good as I thought it should be. So I approached him with the idea of doing events in smaller cities as well as the large cities he was used to. I bugged him about it for six months until he finally relented (probably just to get me off his back). I suggested a "test run" in my hometown of Kamloops (population 85,000). Since he was used to visiting cities with 1,000,000 people or more, this was definitely a big step down for him.

Darren's usual marketing budget in a large city frequently yielded around 300 attendees for the event. For the "Kamloops Experiment," he agreed to invest one-third of his large-city budget. I went to work, did some Kennedy-style marketing, and (to make a long story short) with one-third the normal budget in a city one-tenth the size Darren usually visited, nearly 500 people showed up for the event!

That got his attention, and I quickly became the "Fast Track Marketing Department" by default. My ideas and strategies have helped our database to mushroom by 200% in the last two years and have created a whole new business model. Fast Track has gone from a small company, with only three employees when I started, to a much larger company with over 50 employees at the time of writing this.

Another benefit of becoming someone's "right hand guy" is that it not only gets you instant credibility with that person's database of people (or "herd," as Kennedy calls it), but it also brings in a flow of amazing contacts and deals. You see, a lot of investors and entrepreneurs are actually quite isolated. They are bombarded with business ventures (in other words, a gazillion people are trying to do deals with them), but they don't know where to turn or whom to trust. Chances are, they've been screwed over a few times before. Consequently, if you can show them how you can make their lives easier, more productive, and more profitable—without causing them more work or expense—you become a V.I.P. You get access to the inner workings of some really amazing business deals. You meet some really cool people.

Through my association with Darren Weeks, I have had the privilege of meeting many famous people, including Robert and Kim Kiyosaki and many of the Rich Dad team. I've also met amazing investors and entrepreneurs, including a billionaire who was one of the 25 wealthiest Americans. Drinking a beer in a casual setting with people like this is something most ordinary folks will never get to do.

So, if you like the idea of "leap-frogging" your way to success, and if you are satisfied with being a #2 person like Johnny Carson's Ed McMahon or Batman's Robin, here are my suggested steps:

1. Get to know the person before you pitch them an idea. I had credibility with my star partner ahead of time. I had invested with him. I had gone to his events. I had already shown him that I was serious.

2. It is important to have a very good game plan set up ahead of time. Know exactly what you want to do and what you have to have set up in order to accomplish it. When I approached Darren, I had a very clear idea in my mind of what I wanted to do and how I was going to do it.

3. Make it easy for your prospect to say "yes." When I made my proposition to Darren, I showed him where the profit would come from and how I would do 95% of the work. All he had to do was introduce me to some people, write a monthly article, and help promote the program at his events. I took care of everything else: production, fulfillment, customer service, billing, and collections—absolutely everything else.

4. Make sure that your prospective partner will not be required to put time, money, or reputation at risk. I went out on a limb financially to get the program started. I did not ask my partner for any money, and I bankrolled it until it began to turn a profit.

There you have it. Those are my suggestions for taking a shortcut to success in the information marketing business. Find someone who already has the group and the relationships, and make it worth his or her while to give you access to them, and provide them with a product they want. It's way easier, faster, and cheaper than trying to do it all by yourself.

DAVE DUBEAU is a Canadian entrepreneur who started his first business at age 24 in Costa Rica, Central America. Using Dan Kennedy's strategies he took his company from the bottom of the pack with over 50 competitors into the top three within two years. When he returned to Canada with his Costa Rican wife and family in 2003 Dave had to start all over again. He tried his hand at quick-turn real estate, advertising sales, and marketing consulting. Longing to get involved in information marketing, Dave approached a well-known speaker, "Canadian Rich Dad" Darren Weeks, and proposed doing a joint venture to create a membership program as a part of Darren's business. In two years, the Fast Track Inner Circle grew to over 2,000 members and is over a million dollar a year business and Dave became the marketing director for the Fast Track group of companies.

If you are interested in a Canadian perspective on Robert Kiyosaki's "Rich Dad, Poor Dad" philosophy, you may take a FREE two-month test drive of the Fast Track Inner Circle by visiting www.FTICMembers.com or www.FastTracktoCash-Flow.com.

How to Get Free Publicity to Boost Your Business

DAVID H. WONG, DDS

No matter what type of business you are in, anyone can benefit from publicity. If you are a dentist, carpenter, realtor, carpet cleaner—it does not really matter—you and your business can benefit from publicity. And what is the best type of publicity? Free publicity, of course!

Before we talk about how anyone can get free publicity for his or her business, let's review why you would want publicity in the first place. Do you want to be famous? Do you want to be the expert? The answer to these questions is probably "yes" but let's not forget **the key to survival in any business: Your ability to generate new business and repeat business.** Publicity will help you get both.

When it comes to attracting customers, clients, or patients, nothing is more powerful than a celebrity. Celebrities can influence and sell anything from perfumes to electric grills. Just think George Foreman. Celebrity is so powerful that it can even get you to the governor's mansion like Jesse Ventura or Arnold Schwarzenegger. Celebrities often get more credit than they deserve because the public loves the media. They like rubbing elbows with famous people. They want to be around winners. They like to buy things from celebrities, wear their clothes, and follow their diets, because it gives them a real connection with that celebrity that once only existed through television. Well, what if you are not a celebrity? After all we can't all be famous. That's okay because the next best thing for you is to be "the expert," and anyone can be that. It just takes a little publicity. Think about the doctors featured on reality television like "Dr. 90210" or "Extreme Makeover." Even talk show doctors, like Dr. Phil or Dr. Oz, on "The Oprah Winfrey Show" have reached "expert" status through publicity. That could be YOU.

The great thing about publicity is that not only can it position you as the expert in your field, but it also gives you the type of credibility that you cannot purchase with an advertisement. When you take out an ad, your prospective customers know that it's an ad, and many get on the defensive and immediately tune out your message. Advertisements always cast a shadow of doubt because your prospects are convinced that your ad is just a show or maybe even misleading in some way. When you're on the news or a talk show or in an article, you all of a sudden are more credible. You become real. After all, you're on TV (or radio or print). Why would they put you on TV if you weren't for real? You can present the exact same information that you would in an ad, but the impact on your prospects is so much more powerful and persuasive because you are the expert. You didn't pay for advertising like all of those other businesses. The fact that you do not pay for publicity is what makes it so powerful. The observation that most of your competitors are purchasing ad space and not seeking publicity is the reason why you need to implement a publicity strategy right away.

Why would anyone want to put your business on television, radio, or newspaper? If you're thinking it's because of your talent, looks, or money, you would be dead wrong. If you're good at what you do, congratulations. But that won't get you on TV. When it comes to publicity, it's not about you...it's about the people. If you're going to be on TV, the producers do not care about how many houses you sold last year or that you perform lawn care for the White House. They want to know what you can do for their audience and how they would benefit from what you can give them. They want to know how their audience can save on closing costs or what type of grass to plant in the shade. Do not make the mistake of thinking that your business is not interesting. If you start thinking this, take a look at the newspaper tomorrow. I promise you that your story is way more interesting than several articles in that paper. When it comes to publicity, it really does not matter what business you are in as long as you have the right message. I like to take some advice from Zig Ziglar who says, "You can get whatever it is you want as long as you help enough other people get what they want." This is true in publicity just as it is true in business.

In order to get publicity, everyone needs to master how to write a **press release.** You don't need to hire a public relations company or even need to know the right people. You simply need to learn how to write an effective and interesting press release and get it into the right hands at the right source. Pick out the media you would like to be featured in and go to their website or call and get the e-mail or fax number of the people in charge of getting you on television, radio, newspaper, or any media you desire.

Let's go over what you need to have in your press release.

First of all, your press release should only be one page long. At the top of the page, list your name and contact information in the upper right hand corner. In the upper left hand corner, tell the editor or producer when your story needs to be released. If it can be released at any time, write "For Immediate Release." If your story is time sensitive, write "For Release by _____" and fill in the date. This is common if your story relates to a holiday or a specific event like the presidential election, for example.

Next is the **headline.** This is probably the most critical part of your press release. This is often how initial stories are screened. If you write a bad headline, or even worse, fail to write a headline, your story may get thrown out before it is even read. Your headline should be interesting and make the producer or editor want to read more. A good headline will focus on a benefit that their audience will enjoy by hearing your message. For example, if you are a realtor, you may want to write a headline like "Ten Ways to Sell Your Home in 30 Days or Less." Another good headline could be one that helps readers avoid pain. Going with the realtor example, it could be "Ten Reasons Why Your Home Won't Sell and What to Do About It."

After the headline, your introductory paragraph will explain the headline further. Give a quote or a "sound bite" that explains your story more. Once you have your introduction complete, give a few bullet points that explain what you'll be talking about in your interview. For example, you could have some of the following:

- How your kitchen can turn off buyers

- Four paint colors that are unpopular to 68% of buyers

- The room where you should invest the most money before you sell

The examples are endless. The key with these bullet points is that they do not give anything away. They merely state what you would be talking about and makes the reporter or producer want to call you to find out more. If you make the mistake of giving them the answers in your press release, they may just skip you all together and run the story without you.

Finally, you need to have a closing paragraph that has a line or two about your credentials. Provide your contact information again and gently give any references to your previous publicity appearances.

In total, your press release MUST be no longer than one page. This is crucial. If it is longer than this, you risk getting it thrown out, so make sure it fits on one page only. NO EXCEPTIONS.

A few more tips and hints:

- Make your press release easy to read. Use at least a 12-font size and mix up the look with some **bold type** and *italics.* Use bullet points for an easier read and to draw attention to important points. Don't make the mistake of using small font sizes and single spacing in order to keep your press release to one page; if you have to do this, it is too long. Shorten it!

- Send your press release to as many media sources as you can. You can either fax or e-mail them, but DO NOT call to follow up. This can be a turn off to editors and producers who are too busy to return your phone calls.

- Be ready with a Biography Sheet just in case they want to know more about you. This sheet is actually meant to be about you, so it is okay to talk about you this time.

- Write the questions for them. Reporters and other media people LOVE this. They understand that you know more about your story than they do, so you might as well write the questions. It saves them the time and energy, plus the story will come from an expert's point of view…that is, your point of view!

- Do not be easily discouraged. Not every press release you write is going to get a call back with a reporter wanting to interview you. That's okay. Sometimes they will call within an hour. Sometimes it takes a year. This is why I encourage you to cast a wide net and have several press releases handy.

- Save ALL of your publicity appearances. You can re-use and re-package them over and over for your prospective customers and your current customers as well. Unlike ads, publicity pieces never get old and are always relevant to building your business.

Implementation is the key to getting publicity. Most people are simply too busy or lazy to write their press releases and send them out. As the great Wayne Gretzky once said, "You miss 100% of the shots you don't take." Publicity is cheap, exciting, and fun, but most importantly, it is an effective marketing strategy for growing your business and gaining instant credibility with your customers, clients, or patients. Add this to your marketing plan, and you will separate yourself from your competition.

DR. DAVID H. WONG is a board-certified periodontist who founded GEM Marketing Systems in 2004. The focus of his business is on helping dentists and other healthcare professionals design marketing strategies to maximize profitability. Since 2004, hundreds of businesses have utilized his strategies for new client acquisition, customer retention, sales/case presentations, customer relations, and publicity campaigns. As a dentist, he has used his publicity strategies to make expert appearances on FOX News and in his spare time, he enjoys using his marketing expertise to help publicize charities such as the St. Jude Children's Hospital, the Muscular Dystrophy Association, and the Make a Wish Foundation. Dr. Wong currently practices and resides in Tulsa, Oklahoma with his wife, Jennifer, and their three children.

For sample press releases, a publicity kit, other marketing strategies, and a free newsletter on publicity visit his website: www.GEMmarketingsystems.com. Dr. Wong may also be reached by e-mailing him directly at info@tulsagums. com or faxing 918-749-2924.

How to "Celebrity-ize" Your Business (and Yourself) for Instant Credibility and Star-Powered Publicity

JORDAN MCAULEY

I've always been fascinated with the power of celebrity. When I was younger, I would sometimes write to celebrities letting them know how much I enjoyed their movies or TV shows. Most would write back, including autographed photos, posters, and hand-written letters. I kept track of what contact information worked, and after reading Melvin Power's *How to Get Rich in Mail Order*, started selling my list in small classified ads. This was before the Internet. I charged a few dollars per list, or a book of stamps if the person was like me and didn't yet have a credit card or a checking account. One day I got a letter from a man who wanted to purchase hundreds of my book at a discount for resale. He sent me a check in the mail for $3,000—much to my mother's excitement and horror. And that's when I fell in love with information marketing.

While I can't say I came from rags—both my parents did—and my father made sure I worked. Ever since I can remember he made me have a job—whether it was mowing the grass, cleaning the house, or working as a summer counselor at church camp. We always had nice things growing up—houses, vacations, and cars—but it is to my father's credit that he merely showed us what we could have if we worked hard instead of handing it to us. While it was always difficult watching my friends go to exotic locations on spring break with their father's credit card and later their own trust funds, I'm thankful today that mine made me stay home and work. In fact, he was more concerned that I was working than he was at me getting straight A's in school, which was a good thing because I was much better at my job than I was at school!

My first real job handling money and customers was at a video store in Atlanta during my sophomore year of high school. I was 16. Even after some of my coworkers were held up at gunpoint on three different occasions and therefore quit, I kept working, sometimes late at night by myself, closing the store, and then opening it again the next morning. I worked there for two full years, my junior and senior years of high school. The 1996 Summer Olympic Games came along the summer after I graduated. Wanting to be a part of it, I got a job selling hot dogs and beer. Although the hours were long and I had to wake up early during my last summer before college (4 a.m.!) it was worth it. Not so much to be a part of history, but because I learned that I never want to sell hot dogs or beer again!

After the Olympics, I went off to college at the University of Miami to study film and English. I went in wanting to make movies, but soon learned that movie making wasn't as glamorous as it looked! What I really enjoyed, however, were my marketing and publicity classes. My professors saw that I had a knack for it, and encouraged me to pursue film business instead of production. So that's what I did, ultimately

getting a degree in both Motion Picture Business and English Literature, which is amazing considering how much time I spent building
my business instead of focusing on my classes!

While most of my classmates maybe did one internship, I did three.
The first was in the publicity department of CNN's headquarters in
Atlanta that I got not because of my grades, but because I had started
a business in high school. The second was also in the publicity department at Turner Entertainment the next summer. And the third was
as an agent's assistant at a modeling agency in South Beach my senior
year. I knew that models primarily do one thing—they sell products—
and this interested me. Okay, so working with beautiful people all day
didn't hurt! But it was hard work, especially since I now had to balance
school, my friends, my job, and my business all at the same time.

I had turned Contact Any Celebrity (www.ContactAnyCelebrity.com)
into a complete online business with an email newsletter, membership
site, and my list of celebrity addresses in book form as the Celebrity
Black Book (www.CelebrityBlackBook.com). I had my own merchant
account, was processing credit cards, and taking orders online. Although
at first I catered mostly to autograph seekers, I learned from listening to
my customers that nonprofits, authors, marketers, publicists, and the
media also had a need for my service.

After graduation, I moved to Los Angeles where I landed a job at a
small film production company in Hollywood. I started out making
deliveries all over Los Angeles, which wasn't that fun (if you've been to
L.A. you know how bad the traffic is, and it doesn't help when your
boss is radioing you to hurry!) After doing a couple of odd tasks for a
woman who was in charge of marketing and publicity, she gave me my
own office and a daily list of tasks. Everything from proofreading and

editing her press releases to creating marketing materials and handling her phone calls. I loved it.

Later on the company downsized, and I had to leave that job. But just a few days later I had another, this time as an agent's assistant at a talent agency in Beverly Hills. I read scripts, handled the phones, and got to learn what really gets past the gatekeepers and into celebrities' hands. During this time my Contact Any Celebrity business was continuing to grow. It was hard to justify sitting in an office making $20 an hour when I could be working on my own business, so I left the talent agency, and much to my parent's dismay, told them I was now self-employed.

Today I focus on marketing and publicity, showing authors, experts, and entrepreneurs how to "celebrity-ize" their business—and themselves—for instant credibility and star-powered publicity.

Here are some of my favorite ways:

Create a velvet rope. Velvet ropes always attract attention, create allure, and make people want to get access to whatever it is the rope is protecting. Your velvet rope doesn't have to be physical. Magnolia Bakery in New York City has a "cupcake bouncer" outside, only allowing a certain number of people in at a time to buy cupcakes! Dan Kennedy only accepts communication by fax. Some businesses only accept new clients by referral. You get the idea.

Link yourself to celebrities. Get your photo taken with them whenever you can for your website and marketing materials. I've been photographed with Annie Leibovitz, Paris Hilton, Tim Gunn, Jane Fonda, Nancy Grace, Gene Simmons, and many others. Also, try to have your photograph taken with business leaders and experts who appear at conferences, seminars, trade shows, and speaking engagements.

Get your products in celebrities' hands. Send your products to celebrities in the mail using a service like ContactAnyCelebrity.com to get their addresses. Or place your product in celebrity gift bags and gift suites at award shows and special events. Or give them to celebrity assistants, who may recommend it to their employers, or donate product samples to film and television producers in exchange for screen time and an on-air credit.

"Celebrity-ize" your customers. Your customers crave your attention. Interview and write about them in your newsletter or on your website. Have a "Member of the Month." Invite them to send in video testimonials or even ask them to speak about their success with your business at your events. They'll love the exposure, and you get powerful "live" testimonials.

Use fictional celebrities. How can you use Santa Claus, the Easter Bunny, the Wicked Witch, Cupid, or even Satan? The best part is, these characters are all copyright free. In 2008, Coca-Cola, Palm, iPhone, and Blackberry Storm all used Santa in their ads without paying a dime for licensing.

Provide VIP experiences. Treat your customers like celebrities. Think about how celebrities are treated versus regular customers when they walk into a store or buy something from a company, and aim to treat your customers that way. Provide them with experiences instead of just products and services, and treat all or a premium level of them like VIPs.

Get media attention. I've placed myself, my business, and my employees in local and national broadcast, print, and online media like CNN, *USA Today*, E! Online, *Us Weekly*, *Star Magazine*, *Investor's Business Daily*, *The Wall Street Journal*, *Entrepreneur Magazine*, Bottom Line/Personal, *The Village Voice*, Sirius Satellite Radio, and more. This does wonders for setting you and your business apart from and above the competition.

Hire a celebrity for your event. Having a celebrity at your event not only provides excitement and satisfaction for attendees, it also helps you fill seats. If done right, you can use photo opportunities, media attention, and more to continue promoting your business long after the celebrity has left the stage. You can also hire celebrity impersonators. When I spoke on a panel at Corey Rudl's Wedding Seminar in 2004, he hired a George and Laura Bush impersonator. I thought the guests might feel cheated, but they loved it and it made for a very memorable event.

Use celebrity voices. The Gaylord Opryland Resort in Nashville lets guests choose voices of country singers for their wake up calls. The Nashville Airport uses celebrity voices to get travelers' attention. You can use celebrity voices—real or impersonated—for announcements, invitations, etc. Your voice may be wonderful, but most people won't save your voice mail message and play it for friends, family, and coworkers—no offense! But they most likely will if you use a well-known celebrity's voice.

Write a book and have it published. I started learning about publishing in 1996, when I self-published my first Celebrity Black Book. Since childhood, we are conditioned to respect books. We throw away computer printouts every day, but most of us probably wouldn't throw out a book. We might donate it or give it to someone else, but we wouldn't throw it away. When you publish a book, you become an instant expert, and a celebrity if it sells well.

Known as the "King of Celebrity Contacts," JORDAN MCAULEY is the founder of CELEBRITY PR (www.CELEBRITYPR.com), a media and public relations firm located in New York City that specializes in strategic marketing and publicity services for recognized authors and experts. A graduate of the University of Miami in Motion Picture Business and English Literature from, his record spans more than a decade in publicity, marketing, publishing, events, and entrepreneurship and his Contact Any Celebrity service is one of the most respected publicity resources in the world with billings of more than $1 million annually and a blue-chip roster of over 5,000 marketers, publicists, nonprofits, journalists, and media clients who rely on it daily. He is the author of the best-selling annual directory, the *Celebrity Black Book* (www.CelebrityBlackBook.com), and *Secrets to Contacting Celebrities: 101 Ways to Reach the Rich and Famous*. He lives in New York City where he enjoys power yoga and fancy cupcakes.

For more ways to "celebrity-ize" your business plus a receive a free special report that reveals "How to Get Celebrity Endorsements for Your Products and Services," visit www. CelebrityEndorsements.com today.

In These Tough Economic Times... Flush Your Pipeline and Double Your Sales!

SUE KEYES

The watch sat propped up on the lunch table nearest the window at Rosie's. Every time a loaded coal truck rolled past the window, my dad glanced at the watch. If more than a minute passed between trucks, lunch was short. Off to the tipple to discover what the problems were. My dad knew what it took to make money and a profit in the coal business; he was clear about the numbers and never pretended that problems would fix themselves. Hope was never his business strategy. Your business strategy, like his, needs to include a sales process that allows you to profit.

Profit is not a four-letter word.

Ninety-six percent of my new clients behave as if they were profit averse. They are doing everything in their power to eliminate every opportunity to make a profit. Some of the ways they eliminate profit include:

1. Overpaying the salespeople
2. Keeping salespeople, who can't and wouldn't sell
3. No accountability...the salespeople "do their own thing"

4. No tracking of the sales activities
5. No contact data entered in to a database
6. Letting salespeople "wing it"
7. Expecting salespeople to define and find the prospects
8. Allowing prospects to remain in the pipeline forever
9. Permitting salespeople to continue to follow up with opportunities that will never close
10. Not qualifying the prospects prior to investing the time, resources and money in proposals
11. No clue as to the lifetime value of a client
12. Pennywise and pound foolish with client retention strategies
13. Not tracking or making the right decisions with marketing efforts

Each of the above 13 profit robbers steals some of your success. Any three profit robbers and you'll not be profitable. **All thirteen will kill your business.**

The Profit Robbers 3, 4, 6, 8, 9, and 10 will lead to not closing business chronically. Why do so many sales opportunities never close? Business owners need to know where and when the sale is going to close. They must know what that has to happen for the deals to close. Too often they hope their salespeople know what to do. It's time to stop kidding yourself. Salespeople are human, lazy, and most will do only what they are held accountable to do. Sales is "black magic" for most salespeople, deals close or not and they have no idea of why. Not knowing the why means they will continue to do exactly what they have done before.

Think about it, many people watch movies and miss the lessons. *Paint Your Wagon* is a great movie that will give you a painful reality check about what's happening with your sales. In it, Lee Marvin, a gold miner, observes gold dust, poured out of miner's pouches to pay for drinks. The gold is spilled, knocked to the floor and falls between the cracks. Gold, fallen out of sight is out of mind and lost. Lee makes his livelihood "mining" under all the saloons, collecting the gold that has fallen between the cracks. Are you losing gold between the cracks?

Most of my clients have an out of date, cluttered pipeline of some sort. Recognizing that what my clients had didn't work, the Progression Boards™ was created to capture all the "gold." The Progression Boards™ will protect the profit associated with # 3, 4, 6, 8, 9, and 10. The Progression Boards™ will tell you where to focus your efforts.

Progression Boards™ is a simple, effective system for tracking all sales from lead to qualify to bid, quote, proposal and presentation to close. Designed to give you a clear understanding of exactly what will close, when it will close, the opportunities that will close months from now, and all of your critical numbers, it is based on four different boards. Yes, I recommend physical boards, big ones, which when you stand back, you'll have the complete picture of all of the sales activity for your salespeople. All of your salespeople contribute to the same set of boards. The Progression Boards™ will eliminate hidden facts, fuzzy numbers, or vague reports that will set you up for failure. Nothing for you to fetch! All your salespeople will update the company's Progression Boards™ on a weekly basis. You review it with them weekly. Challenge them on their information and hold them accountable to be accurate.

Lead Board

The first of the Progression Boards™ is the Lead board. On to this board go all prospects: referrals, call ins, responders to direct mail, e-mail, website, trade shows, and ads prospects. Each lead needs the date added and source on the board. Leads are like ripe bananas, good for only a few days. Your number of days will be set by your experience. I have clients whose leads last seven days and I have clients whose leads are only good for one day. To move a prospect off of the lead board it takes an appointment. If an opportunity is to close, what's your ideal way to qualify the prospect? Phone or face to face? How long does it take? What about the prospect that just wants you to put together a proposal without the appointment? How often do they close? Never! Hold your salespeople accountable to follow the process in order to close the deal. Disqualify the prospects that will never close as quickly as possible.

Qualify Board

Now that your have your appointment, move the prospect to the Qualify Board, the second of the Progression Boards™. Qualifying requires that you discover P3, Money and Decision-making. P3 includes the identifying the problems the prospect has, the pain that it is causing them, the financial impact of that pain and their priories in solving the problems. Five different areas of pain are required to close 93% of the opportunities.

Understand your prospects problems, pain, and priorities, then discover how your prospects is going to pay for the solutions. Discover when bills are typically paid and in what timeframe. Colorado Public

Service pays 120 days after service. Wouldn't you want to know that before you put your proposal together?

Your next step is to discover how this decision will be made, both your prospects process for making this kind of decision and who the players are. The CEO/owner is always one of the decision-makers. Answering the 17 qualifier questions will allow you to move on to the Bid, Quote, Proposal and Presentation Board. If the answers indicate a "no close" do not move forward, either qualify or kill the deal.

Bid, Quote, Proposal, and Presentation Board

Prospects that move to this board will close unless you blow this step. The notes you took during your meeting with the prospect will give you the correct language, priority of their problems, budget, and the decision-makers. Present your solution in the order of their priorities. Your Bid, Quote, Proposal, or Presentation Board will include: the gathered information, why you are the best choice for resolving their problems, and "good, better, and best solutions" for their problems. Pricing is included right with each of the "good, better and best solutions." No secrets at this point. Typically, prospects select better with add-ons from the best list. This bid, quote, proposal, or presentation must be delivered live, with the understanding that you'll wait for their decision. Your "yes" prospects will now move to the Close Board.

Close Board

The Close Board tracks the prospects, now opportunities, in their final steps. The number one response to "Why didn't this Opportunity Close" is, "They sent the proposal, but no one ever called me back. No one ever asked me for my business." How much money is waiting for your salespeople just simply to ask for it?

Knowing your critical numbers will allow you to turn on revenue and profit at will. You'll have clear indicators what activity your people need to do. Always start your weekly debriefs with the Close Board; it's the fastest path to cash. Look at your close ratio. How many deals on the Close Board actually close? For example, if you need 10 deals to close each month, and your sales cycle is a month, and if your close ratio is 50% you would need 20 opportunities on the Close Board.

The beauty of the Progression Boards ™ is that they work together to give you a complete picture. Much like with the Close Board, you can figure your ratios for each board. If you need 10 deals to close each month, and your close ratio is 50% you would need 20 opportunities on the Close Board. To get 20 opportunities on the Close Board, you'll need 40 Opportunities on the Bid, Quote, Propose and Present Board, 80 Opportunities on the Qualify Board and 160 Prospects on the Lead Board. If you don't have 160 Leads, you are already in trouble. The reality is it doesn't matter how many sales, what your close ration is, or how long your sales cycle, this system works if you do.

Street Smart Not Ivory Tower

Roll up your sleeves, get your hands on it and take total control of your success. It doesn't matter if you are managing one salesperson or 20. No more fuzzy, phony forecasts. No more pipelines stuffed with opportunities that will never close. Eliminate the "entrepreneurial terror" associated with sales. Stop your gold from falling through the cracks. Implement the Progression Boards™

Peak Performers

Peak performers are a fabulous group of profit-minded business owners who understand the reality of business and are looking for a better way. They are eager to share both successes and failures, so you can learn great resource for getting it done, no excuses! My accomplishments since I joined are many. I achieved in the first quarter of 2008 what I'd achieved in 2007, built a perfect office, wrote a book, *Velcro Management*, created two self-directed CD programs: *If You Knew They Couldn't Sell, Would You Hire Them Anyway?* and *Entrepreneurial Mind Set*.

If this makes sense, STOP reading, go to www.SalesResultsGuaranteeded.com and request the free Progression Boards™ CD. It includes the set up questions, the debrief questions for you to ask your salespeople, and a video of actual debriefings with the Progression Boards™. She can also be reached directly at Sue@SalesResultsGuaranteed.com.

SUZANNE M. KEYES, nicknamed "Trouble," will get you thinking to help you discover what you can be and challenge you to be all you can be. Owner of PHD* Management Group Inc., she is a sales force development expert focused on sales results including top line revenue and bottom line profitability. Sales force development is an integrated approach to grow sales, by improving the people, systems, and strategies with an 18-year track record of client success, which varies from 400% increase in 11 months to 100% growth annually five years running. Sales results require evaluation of the current team, sales training, sales management development, strategic positioning, client retention strategies and hiring correctly. Author of *Velcro Management*, she is the co-author of *Secrets of Peak Performers*. With a history of being a top ten producer nationwide, she is the second woman to ever achieve the Heavy Hitter Award, a top designation of Sandler Sales Institute and the first individual in Colorado to be certified by ISO's CMSI. A proud mother and grandmother, she and her husband live in Centennial, Colorado with their spectacular English springer spaniel puppy, Peyton.

Turn on Your Affiliate Afterburners: 4 Ways to Launch Your Business to Skyrocketing Profitability with Strategic Partners

DAVID FAGAN

Don't underestimate the benefit of affiliates and strategic partners when building your database of leads or your business itself, for that matter. Relationships can be highly profitable when you are able to reach into another person's valuable database and sphere of influence because of his or her endorsement.

To get you started, here are four ways to launch your business to skyrocketing profits:

1) Start with the basics and ask yourself "Who do I already know that I can partner with?" To get the wheels turning use the "wedding principle" in which you ask yourself, "If I were having a wedding, whom would I invite?" Generally, this would include friends, family, and perhaps a few close business associates. What do these wedding guests do for a living? Who are their clients and what circles do they travel in?

You should also be thinking about potential relationship maintenance and profitability. For example, we want people who are high profit and low maintenance and not the other way around. In the beginning you should be willing to work with more people and see if you can train the partners as you set their expectations and serve them. As your time becomes more valuable and your business more established you should also raise your standards for the people with whom you cross-sell.

Any time you start anything new, and at least once a year after that, you should be sending a well-scripted letter out to this "wedding list." The letter should state that, "Although you're new to *(fill in the blank)*, I am very familiar with it and this *(provide a full description)* is what a good referral would look like to me." This sets the stage for a follow-up phone call to discuss a cross-selling relationship and how it could be mutually beneficial. This group won't necessarily be your best source for partners but it's a good start and should not be overlooked. Example: If you offer housecleaning services and your cousin has a heater repair business, you might be able to serve one another's client base. Not a perfect fit, but a good start.

2) The next step builds on the first and starts with the question, "Who do I know who knows who I want to know?" This question is better understood once you realize the importance of fostering and main-taining meaningful relationships for business success. This isn't to say that methods like cold calling or buying lists for direct mail campaigns don't work, especially for getting new clients, but when it comes to strategic partnerships and long-lasting business relationships, they do not produce the best results.

Now, you are either single or you have been single before. When looking for a meaningful personal relationship do you open the white pages to

A and start calling? Then, when someone answers, would you throw out your wish list of measurements and personality traits? Would you go door-to-door telling people about your dream mate? (I sure hope not, but I always come across a few who claim that it may come to that soon!) If you can recognize that this is a terrible way to go about building lasting relationships, then why do so many professionals think this will work in business? The comparison is much closer than you might think.

The next step is to consider who amongst your friends and associates knows the people that you *want* to know. Who can turn that cold lead into a warm one when you drop their name? Who are the best potential affiliates that you can think of for your business?

One great way to come up with a list of key affiliates is to ask, "Which businesses also serve my client base?" If you are in lending, then realtors, contractors, and title companies generally share clients. If you are a website designer, then you most likely share clients with IT consultants, software companies, auto-responder companies, and other e-commerce companies. People in the advising business should have affiliates in other complimentary advice industries. CPA's, attorneys, insurance professionals, financial advisers, lenders and realtors can all be good sources of leads if you are in the advice business, but you need to go deeper than that.

Now that you are getting ready to blast off, ask yourself, "Who do I know that knows people in these businesses?" Then get in touch and ask if you can reference them. Better yet, ask them to give you an introduction.

For example, we at Infusionsoft have been fans of Jay Conrad Levinson, the "Guerilla Marketing Guru," for quite some time, but until recently we didn't have a connection with this worldwide best-seller. Eventually, we found that Jeff Liesener at High Achievers knew a key member of Jay's team, Todd Beeler. Introductions were made, e-mails were exchanged, and within days I was not only working with Guerilla Marketing, but was given expert status thanks to a great recommendation from Jeff. Six weeks later I was speaking at one of Jay's events in Orlando, which led to strategic brainstorming with Jay himself after he heard me speak. So it's true that it's not always what you know, but who you know that gets you ahead.

Once you start meeting with these potential partners, make sure you're asking questions to find out what they want in a "perfect partner" so that you can customize a solution to fit their needs.

I have been approached several times by people who don't know anything about me, or my business, but will immediately begin spewing out information that is useless to me. Sales expert and author Todd Duncan calls this the "show up and throw up" approach. Remember, the approach will work best if it your approach is centered around the affiliate's needs rather than your own.

3) Start serving the right people right away. Zig Ziglar says, "In order to get what you want, you need to help other people get what they want." However, it's important that you not just give without thinking, but that you offer something of value.

The more successful the partner, the more influential and valuable you need to be in order to get their attention. For instance, if you are fairly new to the business world you are probably not going to get Donald Trump or Oprah Winfrey to return your call. Even if you have that warm referral and get the call answered you have to be able to convey what you bring to the table besides a fork and knife. Think about building your product and service in such a way that it can really serve potential business partners and their clients, in order to achieve maximum impact for you.

For example, we at Infusionsoft have been very fortunate to work with Dan Kennedy and Bill Glazer, known to many as GKIC or Peak Performers. However, I know that we would never have developed a successful partnership with GKIC if Infusionsoft had not enabled Dan Kennedy and Bill Glazer to help so many of their own clients grow their businesses. Sure, Dan and Bill like what we do for them, but they love what we do for their loyal clients. In the end, what works is a partnership that is strategic for both parties involved.

In August of 2008, Infusionsoft created, facilitated, and ultimately drove a four-city tour to a successful $400,000 power play in just eight weeks with Dan Kennedy. The tour put us in four cities in four days thanks to blood, sweat, tears, and a private jet. Maybe that's a little melodramatic, but despite the hectic schedule it was truly a win-win for everyone involved, including the attendees. Did I mention Dan also sold over a thousand books and helped his clients get closer to their dream of financial freedom? Maybe now you see just what I mean by turning on the affiliate afterburners that will launch your business to skyrocketing profitability. How will your unique selling proposition serve your affiliates' clients? How will you serve your affiliates? Figuring that out is half the battle.

4) **Lastly, make it easy for your affiliates to work with you and get paid.** You need to account for campaign marketing copy in addition to

graphics, perhaps website landing pages and the exchange of revenue. All of these things are your responsibility and must be proactively provided for your strategic partners, so they don't have to think about it and it doesn't slow you down. Obviously I am a little biased, but affiliate tracking is one of the things that Infusionsoft technology does better than anyone else. You would be crazy not to speak with us about managing your affiliate program! Of course, I really don't care how you do it, as long as the process gets automated quickly. Do it for your affiliates' sake, if not for your own.

For example, we made the four-city tour with Dan Kennedy really easy. We scheduled the hotels, we created the copy (Dan definitely gave us his feedback, which we appreciated), we sent out the email campaigns, we booked the jet, we created the landing pages, we created the follow-up sequences, and we brought the manpower necessary to make that tour a success.

We at Infusionsoft understand and value our affiliates more than any other company that I know. All of our clients become affiliates and we track this process to perfection. Our big affiliates or strategic partners include Mark Victor Hansen, Michael Gerber, Perry Marshall, Joel Comm, T. Harv Eker, Ron LeGrand, Alexis Neeley, Joe Polish, Rich Schefren, Sean Greeley, Yanik Silver, Matt Bacak, Jay Abraham, and Alex Mandossian, just to name a few. These high-level affiliates make up 40 percent of our business and contributed to the $10 million in venture capital we received at the end of 2007. I am confident that they will also be a significant force in driving Infusionsoft toward household name status for small businesses worldwide.

Don't underestimate what the right affiliates can do for your business, when you help them grow their business first. You don't even have to take my word for it, just look at the success of Infusionsoft at more than 1,000 percent growth in the last year, thanks in large part to our affiliates!

DAVID FAGAN LEE loves to teach and inspire others to reach their full business potential. Years of experience presenting in public, hosting a radio show, and motivating on stage developed David's skills for effectively communicating with an audience. His real passion is for the sales team, small business owner, and entrepreneur. He is an open book willing to share his successes as well as his failures. After five years at a big bank, David embraced his own entrepreneurial spirit and purchased an existing company. He grew that business into several offices across multiple states and had a team of 200 salespeople reporting to him. While still continuing his coaching and speaking engagements David joined Infusionsoft, an Inc. 500 company helping to revolutionize the way small businesses grow. As a business development coach, David plays an integral role in building Infusionsoft's strategic partner network. If you want to develop a winning sales plan as well as automate it, then there is no one better to work with than David Fagan Lee and Infusionsoft. He has completed Harvard's program on negotiation and has been awarded with a professional membership to the National Speakers Association. He currently resides in Mesa, Arizona with his wife and six children.

Hire with Certainty

KEVIN CONNELL

S ue Weaver and I had many things in common, we both enjoyed playing golf, each of us had left the corporate world in 1994 to became entrepreneurs, our companies were head-quartered in Florida. Sue's company, Embroidery Concepts, Inc., was just up the I-4 corridor in Orlando, about an hour's drive away from me in Tampa. We both had loving families and a great circle of friends. Both of us lived a life with passion, until the day when it all changed…

Sue Weaver was raped and beaten to death in her home; her killer then set fire to it with the goal of destroying any evidence that would link him to the crime. What makes this story even more tragic is that it was preventable.

Sue had received a savings coupon to have the air conditioning ducts cleaned in her home, she responded to the advertisement from Bur-dine's Department Stores. What Sue did not know was that both of the men sent to her home to perform the job were convicted felons, and one of the men, Jeffrey Hefling, was a twice-convicted sex offender, who at one point in the judicial system, was sentenced to life in prison. Yet Hefling, who was out on parole, was hired to perform service work in people's homes allowing him access to victimize again.

The company that hired Hefling settled a $9 million dollar negligent hiring lawsuit brought by Sue Weaver's family. The criminal courts eventually took care of Hefling, who has since been convicted of the rape and murder of Sue, and is now serving a life sentence at Gulf Correctional Institute in Florida. Adler Services Inc., a former subcontractor of Burdines and the company that hired Hefling, never conducted a background check before hiring him.

Generally, an employer may be liable to third parties for failure to exercise ordinary care in selecting responsible, competent employees or, if an employer retains an employee who it knew or should have known was unfit for the position in which the employee was placed.

In a negligent hiring or retention case, the plaintiff will likely focus on the fact that the employee should not have been hired and that the employer failed to verify references, inquire as to any criminal record, or notice gaps in employment history. This was the case with Sue Weaver as were the negligent hiring cases cited below:

In Harrison v. Tallahassee Furniture Co., Inc., there was a $2 million judgment against the employer. The furniture company hired a worker without doing a background check on him. After hours, the employee violently attacked and severely injured a store customer to whom he had made a delivery several days before the assault.

In McKishnie v. Rainbow International Carpet Dyeing and Cleaning Co., the award was a $1.8 million judgment against the employer. A carpet cleaning franchise hired a worker without completing a background check. The worker lied on his application regarding reasons for leaving his prior employment and had been fired by a previous employer for being arrested for a violent crime. After he was hired, he strangled two female University of Florida students in their apartment when he became angry over the students' request that he move some furniture before he cleaned the carpet.

Most employers know that they can significantly reduce risk and improve the quality of employees by doing a thorough background check on applicants before hiring, yet the overwhelming majority of employers don't do them, or they don't do them correctly. Many don't even check references. Why?

There are two main reasons:

1. **They think "disaster" only happens to the other guy.** This is how the horror stories and scandals you hear about in the news – like the Sue Weaver Case – happen. Employee theft, embezzlement, falsification of resumes, drug use, and more affect a large percentage of both blue collar and white collar populations. It's natural to think these bad apples find their way only into other peoples' yards. We like to think the best of people.

2. **They don't have time.** Doing background checks requires skills, knowledge, and ready access to information most business owners don't have. Just verifying the information provided on applications and in resumes takes too much time.

Here's why these things are so important TO YOU:

Your failure to check into criminal histories may lead to your hiring a thief, embezzler, or even violent criminals, such as a rapist. Not only could you suffer losses from disruption of your business or theft, but you could also be open to negligence lawsuits from other employees

or customers robbed or assaulted by the employee. Think it couldn't happen to you and wipe out all you've worked for? Think again.

Failure to verify Social Security numbers could get you in trouble with the IRS, the Social Security Administration, US Citizenship and Immigration, and Homeland Security.

Failure to verify past employment as well as licenses could put an employee in your business who is not qualified to do the work, or worse, not licensed and legally able to do the work – leaving you open to fines or litigation.

Failure to look into criminal history, bad credit situations, etc. sharply increases your risk of theft or embezzlement by employees. From 1998 to 2007, embezzlement has grown by $200 billion. Further, employees with access to your customers' credit card data and other private information can steal from your customers – but you can be held liable. If you were negligent in your hiring practices, you'll have no defense.

Our analysis, in screening for many corporations for the past 15 years, indicates that 43% of applicants lie about something on their resume or job application. Even if your small office, store, or restaurant hires as few as three people a year, the odds say you are likely to be hiring someone based on false information without comprehensive background screening. NO ONE should hire anybody without these defensive measures.

It is not uncommon for high-ranking industry professionals and corporate chiefs to exaggerate or even make up credentials when they apply for a job. Resume fraud stories are commonplace today, George O'Leary, former Head Football Coach of Notre Dame, Dave Edmonson, former CEO of Radio Shack and Marilee Jones, former MIT Dean of Admissions are three cases that received international attention for resume lies. In fact, the FBI estimates that more than 500,000 people nationwide claim college degrees they never earned.

Recently, I was a guest on the *ABC News* business television program "Money Matters," where I was interviewed about some of the most outrageous resume lies that I have come across in my 15 years as CEO of AccuScreen.com.

The Top 7 Resume Lies:

1. Dates of Employment

2. Job Title or Rank

3. Criminal Records

4. Inflated Salary

5. Education (e.g. Bogus Degrees – Diploma Mills)

6. Professional Licenses (e.g. MD, RN, CPA, etc.)

7. "Ghost" Companies (e.g. self-owned fictional company)

Source: www.accuscreen.com, overall ranking 1994-2007

If a company does not verify the past history of their job applicants, and knowing that well over one-third of all job applications are falsified, the company inevitably will be hiring a problem employee or what I refer to as a "ticking time bomb" that could go off at anytime. Thoroughness is most important. The problem exists; it is out there and it's not going to go away! It is only human nature to try to ignore it. Fraud and deceit in hiring as well as workplace violence are not myths. They are real and growing problems.

There are several simple rules that employers must follow before implementing background checks to ensure that their company is not exposed to potential liability. Put in the time to examine your needs and recruit and hire in a systematic, legal way. Then institute a policy as a major corporate goal, giving it wide distribution among employees.

Recognizing that laws vary from state to state, below are options that may be available to you for background checks on prospective employees:

- Criminal history search

- Sexual offender/predator inquiry

- Social security number trace

- Motor vehicle/driving record check

- Terrorist watch list

- Drug testing

- Education verification

- Credit report

- Professional license verification

- Prospective partner or vendor background check

Sound complicated? It is! Many companies turn this task over to an outside professional screening service, which offers various advantages. They serve as an independent third party, there is no "halo" effect, and the systems and staff are in place to give you a quick turnaround time.

Whether starting a new program or continuing an old one, get the complete, accurate, objective picture before making a hiring decision. As in all company policies, seek the advice of attorneys or other experts before deciding on the exact language to use. Take into account federal and state laws, the nature of your business, and any practices that have guided you in the past.

The *problem* is that hiring personnel is a serious process with serious implications for the future of your business. The solution is to reduce the risk by getting the vital information needed about a potential employee when you need it – *before* hiring!

The information contained is intended for informational purposes only and does not constitute specific advice. Employers should consult competent legal counsel before implementing a program.

KEVIN G. CONNELL received his bachelor's in economics management from Ohio Wesleyan University, graduating Summa Cum Laude and Phi Beta Kappa. He is founder and chief executive officer of Accu-Screen, Inc., www.accuscreen.com, headquartered in Tampa, Florida, which provides pre-employment background screening services worldwide. He is a nationally known speaker, author, and frequent radio and TV guest, having appeared on over 72 radio and TV Programs, sharing his expertise and insights on effective employment screening practices. He has been on the adjunct faculty of the University of South Florida since 1998, where he teaches the course Effective Employee Screening. He recently served as a director with National Association of Professional Background Screeners where he was elected by his peers to serve on the Board of Directors and has twice provided testimony before the Florida Supreme Court on criminal record background checks and safety in the workplace.

Kevin Connell is Founder & CEO of Accu-Screen, Inc. www.accuscreen.com which has been providing background checks on prospective and current employees since 1994. Readers of this book may receive a complimentary copy of Insider Secrets of Criminal Background Checks (a $247.00 Value) by visiting www.accuscreen.com/topsecret, or you may call to request it, (800) 689-2228.

Inspecting What You Expect: 7 Ways to Verify Your Team Is Doing What You Want

CHRIS MULLINS

The "7 Ways to Verify Your Team Is Doing What You Want" are wealth building and productivity strategies. Training tools adaptable to any business of any size selling services and products to inspect what you expect, which is the exceptional "Wow Experience." You get to experience what your customers experience, imagine that!

Disney has kiosks and stands called "listening posts" throughout the park with the sole intention of listening to customers. We support and recommend "listening posts" and "viewing posts" of a different kind. You'll learn more about this as you read on.

We teach clients that customer service is sales, sales is customer service; upselling is customer service and communication of all types is sales which creates the relationship and experience.

Imagine a team of expert skilled professionals looking over the business owner and manager's shoulders, being there when you can't to hear actual sales (case) presentations (remember, all customer communication is selling) from the receptionist to customer service to inside sales to help desks to call centers. Whether you're a franchise owner in the karate business or restaurants or retail stores, high-end dentists to an affluent market, chiropractors in professional practice, architect, a cosmetic surgeon, a well heeled barber shop, automotive repair, healthcare, tax preparation, veterinarian, pest control, or even a dance studio (any business), you just can't be there all the time. What a fantastic opportunity to train and recognize your team, to identify the diamonds in the bunch that really shine (as well as those that may be in the wrong job), and to fix problem areas that are losing you hundreds of thousands of dollars each year.

1. Workplace Video and Audio Surveillance Cameras are exceptional training and compliance tools for all business owners. However, like many shiny new gadgets, business owners invest in this technology and then don't use it. Our team can get this done for you with the help of our experts. Horror Story: The director of a large corporation went out of town and came back to the office only to find some items stolen. I asked him, "Don't you have surveillance cameras you can watch?" He replied, "Yes, but I'm not going to watch 14 hours of it; I know who it was."

You want to be up front when you install the cameras. Tell your team why this is part of the culture at your business now; this is an ongoing training tool. Through this process, of course, you'll also uncover important information that will help you to make better decisions on individuals that aren't a match for your business. You'll be able to perfect your hiring practices. Imagine for a moment how valuable this staff-training tool would be for improving your bottom line, sales, customer interaction, relationship building, experience, and marketing.

You can watch in real time what's happening with your business from your laptop anywhere, anytime.

This is a bottom line business-training tool. You'll be able to see how your team reacts to customers, how customers react to your team, what's the response time and their body language. For the absentee business owner this is invaluable. You'll know where your team is, and you can even use it as a way to perfect the in-person sales presentation. You'll identify who's servicing the customer, who's talking on a cell phone in the corner, who's taking breaks, who's chewing gum while talking to customers, etc. Ultimately, you'll know if you have a "sales prevention team" or "sales opportunity team."

2. Mystery Calls Playing Prospect. Here are a couple of horror stories we've uncovered with our program. The receptionist at a pest control company takes the call and yells out as she goes to make the transfer, "I have a beast of a woman on the phone." Here's another, an automotive repair shop that says, "Go down the street to my buddy's shop. He's our competitor but his reception area is much nicer." Or, the receptionist at a dental office, "It's too far for you to drive; I'll just send you some information." By the way, the owners of these businesses told me personally, "These are my best people, one being with the owner for 10 years, my right hand guy." Every once in a while we get a client that says, "Are you sure that was my office? We would never say something like that." And that's after they hear the recording! Oy!

Put a system in place where you're calling the office with organized "scripted" scenarios. Be sure your team knows you're doing mystery calls as part of your training program and share the results. How does your team handle the call from the time they greet the caller (which is the very start of the relationship building experience) to the transfer and all the way to the next person? Pay close attention to the language used, the tone of voice, and pauses. If you've developed a script (we don't teach students to sound like robots, but we do support scripts as your roadmap to keeping customers and closing sales) you can monitor if it's working and if it's being used. This is a great hiring tool.

3. A Web-Based Telephone Monitoring System to measure, track, and record inbound and outbound phone calls. It doesn't get better than this. Why do mystery calls when you can set up "listening posts" of real calls? You'll be able to know how your team is talking to new and established customers. Automatically track the number of incoming calls for an accurate return on investment (ROI) on your marketing lead generation dollars and red flags. You'll be able to measure the length of calls, which will tell you if your team knows your products and services, and if they're going off script saying too much or too little. You'll also get alerts on dropped calls and you can quickly identify why they were dropped.

Set up "listening posts" for every department in your business because all forms of communication with your prospects and established customers are "sales moments" that can keep the RELATIONSHIP and EXPERIENCE strong and moving forward or can STOP IT ABRUPTLY. Without "listening posts" and "viewing posts" you won't know why it stopped and will never be able to fill the holes in your bucket, let alone identify what works and what doesn't.

You're spending hundreds of thousands of dollars to create a marketing program to get your phone to ring, to get your prospects and customers to visit your business. How do you know it's happening the way you want?

4. Phone Success Training and Coaching Programs. Continuing education, especially at all customer entrance points into your business from the telephone to face-to-face, is a must to create long lasting habits and behaviors that are congruent with your customer experience sales goals. It's not your team's fault that they may not be doing everything the way you want, because in many cases you didn't tell them how to do it. You didn't provide them the tools or hold them accountable for using the tools you do provide.

Involve your team in your marketing plans, training them on the different programs you offer so when prospects and customers call and visit your business, the team knows exactly what enticed them to take the step and can communicate your specific goals. Include the checklist, the steps, the script that you want your team to take, and then launch your program—it's "script rehearsal" time. We teach businesses how to do their own internal training or, conversely, we can do it.

How do you know if your team is getting it, that they understand all that you direct them to do if you don't get involved with them and if you don't provide ongoing training and coaching? It's critical to experience what your customers' experience, whether by "listening posts" (monitoring phone calls), "viewing posts" (surveillance cameras) or in-person mystery shopping. These methods are the absolute best way to fix the disasters that are about to occur. The best turnkey training tools and services are available to you and we can show you how to use them—or we can do it for you. Inspecting what you expect is the best way to uncover hidden secrets to helping your customers.

Inspecting what you expect in your business—with regards to the customer experience by telephone or in person—is the best way to uncover and fix financial nightmares that are happening. This is an also an incredible training opportunity to help your entire team and your business grow quickly.

5. Online Chat Customer Service. Play prospective chat customer and see what the experience is like. Are you going to get sales from this service? What type of language is being used? Are your scripts being followed? What's the response time? Learn about your marketing opportunities. How do you know unless you play customer?

6. Web Site Mystery Shopping. Put a system in place to "play" customer on your website and check out all your different services and products. Is it easy to navigate? What's it like to ask questions? What about placing orders? What's the EXPERIENCE like on your website?

7. Mystery Shopping In-Person. Is your business everything you say it is? You'll be able to check the appearance of your staff. Are their aprons and shirts ironed? Are there holes in armpits when they stretch? Bad breath? Coffee all over the front of their shirt? Are they yawning constantly? Chewing gum? Smelling like cigarettes? The bathroom? Horror story: You're waiting in line at a fast food restaurant. The French fry cook is tossing fries while yelling on a cell phone tucked in her shoulder, "I'll send the police over there if you don't get out!" Even churches have what they call "mystery worshippers" providing a laundry list of imperfections. Why wouldn't you do this in your own business?

Being a peak performer has significantly added huge revenue growth to my business and aligned me with entrepreneurs at the top of their game in today's business to learn from year after year from our group meetings, mastermind sessions, coaching calls, and ongoing networking. Like everything in life, you get out of it exactly what you put into it. Peak performers are trained and coached to take action and hold each other accountable.

Chris Mullins is the Phone Sales Doctor "Inspecting What You Expect" and CEO of Mullins Media Group™, LLC, a company that provides skilled mystery shopping by phone, analysis of calls, scripting, staff phone training, ongoing compliance of handling calls and customer interaction, properly providing full-scale workplace video audio surveillance cameras, web-based telephone monitoring systems and in-person mystery shopping programs. He attacks a significant problem area with regards to customer experience, the handling of inbound calls, and face-to-face customer interaction. Go to www.MullinsMediaGroup.com for more information and a free offer.

OFFER # 1: www.GreatBottomLine.com for FREE Money-Making How-To Telephone Skills Reports. Be sure to include "PEAK BOOK sent me."

OFFER # 2: One 15-Minute Telephone Consult with Chris to discuss your business schedule by FAXING 603-924-5770 and include your complete contact information. Be sure to include "PEAK BOOK sent me."

The Most Incredible FREE Gift Ever

($613.91 Worth of Pure Money-Making Information)

Dan Kennedy & Bill Glazer are offering an incredible opportunity for you to see WHY <u>Glazer-Kennedy Insider's Circle</u>^{TM} is known as "THE PLACE" where entrepreneurs seeking FAST and Dramatic Growth and greater Control, Independence, and Security come together. Dan & Bill want to give you **$613.91 worth of pure Money-Making Information** including TWO months as an 'Elite' Gold Member of Glazer-Kennedy's Insider's Circle^{TM}. You'll receive a steady stream of MILLIONAIRE Maker Information including:

* Glazer-Kennedy University: Series of 3 Webinars (Value = $387.00)

The 10 "BIG Breakthroughs in Business Life *with Dan Kennedy*
- HOW <u>Any</u> Entrepreneur or Sales Professional can Multiply INCOME by 10X
- **HOW to Avoid Once and for All being an *"Advertising Victim"***
- The "*Hidden Goldmine*" in Everyone's Business and HOW to Capitalize on it
- **The BIGGEST MISTAKE most Entrepreneurs make in their Marketing**
- And the <u>BIGGEE</u>…Getting Customers Seeking You Out.

The ESSENTIALS to Writing Million Dollar Ads & Sales Letters BOTH Online & Offline *with Marketing & Advertising Coach, Bill Glazer*
- How to INCREASE the Selling Power of <u>All</u> Your Advertising by Learning the <u>13 "Must Have" Direct Response Principles</u>
- **Key Elements that Determine the Success of Your Website**
- HOW to Craft a Headline the Grabs the Reader's Attention
- **How to Create an Irresistible Offer that Melts Away <u>Any</u> Resistance to Buy**
- The <u>Best</u> Ways to Create Urgency and Inspire IMMEDIATE Response
- ***"Insider Strategies"* to INCREASE Response that you <u>Must</u> be using both ONLINE & Offline**

The ESSENTIALS of Productivity & Implementation for Entrepreneurs *w/ Peak Performance Coach Lee Milteer*
- How to Almost INSTANTLY be MORE Effective, Creative, Profitable, and Take MORE Time Off
- **HOW to Master the "Inner Game" of Personal Peak Productivity**
- How to Get MORE Done in Less Time
- **HOW to Get Others to Work On <u>Your</u> Schedule**
- How to Create Clear Goals for SUCESSFUL Implementation
- And Finally the BIGGEE…How to Stop Talking and Planning Your Dreams and Start Implementing Them into Reality

* 'Elite' Gold Insider's Circle Membership (Two Month Value = $99.94):

- Two Issues of *The NO B.S. Marketing Letter:*

  Each issue is at least 12 pages – usually MORE – Overflowing with **the latest Marketing & MoneyMaking Strategies**. Current members refer to it as <u>a day-long intense seminar in print</u>, arriving by first class mail every month. There are ALWAYS terrific examples of *"What's-Working-NOW"* **Strategies**, timely Marketing news, trends, ongoing teaching of <u>Dan Kennedy's Most IMPORTANT Strategies</u>… and MORE. As soon as it arrives in your mailbox you'll want to find a quiet place, grab a highlighter, and devour every word.

- Two CDs Of The **EXCLUSIVE GOLD AUDIO INTERVIEWS**

  These are EXCLUSIVE interviews with <u>successful users of direct response advertising, leading experts and entrepreneurs in direct marketing, and famous business authors and speakers.</u> Use them to turn commuting hours into "POWER Thinking" hours.

* The New Member No B.S. Income Explosion Guide & CD (Value = $29.97)

This resource is <u>especially designed for NEW MEMBERS</u> to show them HOW they can join the thousands of Established Members **creating exciting sales and PROFIT growth** in their Business, Practices, or Sales Careers & Greater SUCCESS in their Business lives.

Income Explosion FAST START Tele-Seminar with Dan Kennedy, Bill Glazer, and Lee Milteer (Value = $97.00)

Attend from the privacy and comfort of your home or office…hear a DYNAMIC discussion <u>of Key Advertising, Marketing, Promotion, Entrepreneurial & Phenomenon strategies</u>, PLUS answers to the most Frequently Asked Questions about these Strategies

* You'll also get these Exclusive "Members Only" Perks:

- **Special FREE Gold Member CALL-IN TIMES:** Several times a year, Dan & I schedule Gold-Member ONLY Call-In times
- **Gold Member RESTRICTED ACCESS WEBSITE**: Past issues of the *NO B.S. Marketing Letter*, articles, special news, etc.
- **Continually Updated MILLION DOLLAR RESOURCE DIRECTORY** with Contacts and Resources Dan & his clients use.

To activate your MOST INCREDIBLE FREE GIFT EVER you only pay a one-time charge of $19.95 (or $39.95 for Int'l subscribers) to cover postage (this is for everything). **After your 2-Month FREE test-drive, you will automatically continue at the <u>lowest</u> Gold Member price of $49.97 per month ($59.97 outside North America). Should you decide to cancel your membership, you can do so at any time by calling Glazer-Kennedy Insider's Circle™ at 410-825-8600 or faxing a cancellation note to 410-825-3301 (Monday through Friday 9am – 5pm). Remember, your credit card will NOT be charged the low monthly membership fee until the beginning of the 3rd month, which means you will receive 2 full issues to read, test, and profit from all of the powerful techniques and strategies you get from being an Insider's Circle Gold Member. And of course, it's impossible for you to lose, because if you don't absolutely LOVE everything you get, you can simply cancel your membership before the third month and never get billed a single penny for membership.**

***EMAIL REQUIRED IN ORDER TO NOTIFY YOU ABOUT THE
GLAZER-KENNEDY UNIVERSITY WEBINARS AND FAST START TELESEMINAR***

Name _____ Business Name _____

Address _____

City _____ State _____ Zip _____ e-mail* _____

Phone _____ Fax_____

Credit Card Instructions to Cover $19.95 for Shipping & Handling:

_____Visa _____MasterCard _____ American Express _____ Discover

Credit Card Number _____ Exp. Date _____

Signature _____ Date _____

Providing this information constitutes your permission for Glazer-Kennedy Insider's Circle™ to contact you regarding related information via mail, e-mail, fax, and phone.

**FAX BACK TO 410-825-3301
Or mail to: 401 Jefferson Ave., Towson, MD 21286
www.PeakPerformersGift.com**

TreeNeutral

Advantage Media Group is proud to be a part of the Tree Neutral™ program. Tree Neutral offsets the number of trees consumed in the production and printing of this book by taking proactive steps such as planting trees in direct proportion to the number of trees used to print books. To learn more about Tree Neutral, please visit **www. treeneutral.com**. To learn more about Advantage Media Group's commitment to being a responsible steward of the environment, please visit **www.advantagefamily.com/green**